S. Hrg. 115–75

CULTURAL SOVEREIGNTY SERIES: MODERNIZING THE INDIAN ARTS AND CRAFTS ACT TO HONOR NATIVE IDENTITY AND EXPRESSION

FIELD HEARING

BEFORE THE

COMMITTEE ON INDIAN AFFAIRS
UNITED STATES SENATE

ONE HUNDRED FIFTEENTH CONGRESS

FIRST SESSION

JULY 7, 2017

Printed for the use of the Committee on Indian Affairs

U.S. GOVERNMENT PUBLISHING OFFICE

26–821 PDF   WASHINGTON : 2017

For sale by the Superintendent of Documents, U.S. Government Publishing Office
Internet: bookstore.gpo.gov   Phone: toll free (866) 512–1800; DC area (202) 512–1800
Fax: (202) 512–2104   Mail: Stop IDCC, Washington, DC 20402–0001

CONTENTS

CULTURAL SOVEREIGNTY SERIES: MODERNIZING THE INDIAN ARTS AND CRAFTS ACT TO HONOR NATIVE IDENTITY AND EXPRESSION

FRIDAY, JULY 7, 2017

U.S. SENATE,
COMMITTEE ON INDIAN AFFAIRS,
Santa Fe, NM.

The Committee met, pursuant to notice, at 10:17 A.M. in the Santa Fe Indian School gymnasium, Hon. Tom Udall, Vice Chairman of the Committee, presiding.

OPENING STATEMENT OF HON. TOM UDALL, U.S. SENATOR FROM NEW MEXICO

Senator UDALL. Well, first of all, welcome to everybody today. It's wonderful to have you here, and it's wonderful to be at this location. I'll talk about that a little bit further on, but I want to have welcoming remarks by Roy Herrera, superintendent of the Santa Fe Indian School, who is our great and generous host today. Thank you very much, Roy, for being here and being our host.

Mr. HERRERA. Thank you, Senators and guests, for being here at the Santa Fe Indian School. My name is Roy Herrera. I'm the superintendent of the Santa Fe Indian School. On behalf of our board of directors, board of trustees, our students, our staff, I would like to welcome you to this campus, beautiful campus here in Santa Fe. Also, I want to thank you for being here today, and anything that we can do here at Santa Fe Indian School to increase your stay—better stay, we'd appreciate it.

Thank you, Senators.

Senator HEINRICH. You're welcome.

Senator UDALL. Roy, thank you. Thank you so much for that welcome. And I would next like to recognize Marvin Trujillo. Marvin is a Marine Corps officer and Native veteran, and Marvin's going to recognize us in a prayer. Is that correct? Are you doing the Pledge of Allegiance?

Marvin's doing the Pledge of Allegiance. We'll all rise and take our hats off.

[Pledge of Allegiance recited.]

Thank you, Marvin. Marvin, thank you for that, and thank you for your service to our country. We really appreciate that.

And now we're going to stand again and recognize Santa Fe Indian School student Jude Chavarria from the Santa Clara Pueblo to offer the opening prayer.

[Opening prayer recited.]

Senator UDALL. Thank you, Jude, so much, for that prayer. We really appreciate you giving that this morning.

And good morning. I call this hearing to order. Let me first, before we start with our panelists and our opening statements, I'd like to acknowledge the former chairman of the Committee, this Committee, this Senate Indian Affairs Committee, Senator Ben Nighthorse Campbell. He just happens to be in town, Senator Campbell. He was here, traveled down, and he saw it in the paper that we were holding this hearing. He has a lot of experience on this issue, extensive knowledge as an author of the Act. But he's also a Native American jeweler himself. Look at that wonderful bolo tie he's wearing. I'm sure he's the one that created that.

So Senator Campbell, I would ask you to come to the podium here. I wanted to have you give brief remarks before we did the opening and just talk to us about your experience and what you learned.

So thank you for being here. As he's making it over to the podium, I just want to say, when I started serving in the House, Senator Campbell was a Republican; I was a Democrat. But we always had lunch once a month, and we tried to do everything we could to work through these issues, Western issues, which he cared very much about.

So Senator Campbell, please. The microphone is yours.

STATEMENT OF HON. BEN NIGHTHORSE CAMPBELL, U.S. SENATOR (RETIRED) FROM COLORADO

Senator CAMPBELL. Thank you, Mr. Chairman. And by the way, thank you for complimenting me on my bolo. I didn't make it.

It is from a good friend who unfortunately passed away from a motorcycle accident by the name of Singer, Tommy Singer. He was a Navajo, a well-known Navajo silversmith. He made this some years ago, and I cherish it because he was a good friend. But thank you for the compliment. And as you mention, I'm kinda here by accident, so I don't have any prepared statement.

But, by the way, I'm Northern Cheyenne on my dad's side. Since the 1970s, my wife and I have lived on the Southern Ute reservation in Southwest Colorado right near Mesa Verde in some other historic and mystical places that you should come and visit.

But I've been involved in jewelry ever since I was a boy, starting in 1945, if you can imagine that. That will tell you how old I am. In those days, we made everything from coins. We'd go down and put them on a railroad track. We were always on the wrong side of the track when we were kids and poor.

We never made any money from them. We used to trade them for food. In those days, everybody was poor. Everybody. So it's not like I was the only one that kinda came up the hard way.

But I was pretty active in helping revise the 1990 Act, and I'd like to maybe venture a little bit about the things I think were good about it and maybe things that still need to be addressed.

Bill Richardson and I who was the last-elected Governor of New Mexico, as you know, but we were on the Committee of Interior and Insular Affairs when Senator Udall, Mo Udall, was the chairman. His dad, by the way, about that time was Secretary of Interior. So our families kinda go way back.

Bill and I recognized some of the things that were happening with the plagiarism of American Indian art, particularly in jewelry. So the first bill that we tried to get introduced was a bill that would require all, quote/unquote, Indian jewelry made in China and Japan, and all over the place, it was made here to be stamped in the metal, point of origin stamped in the metal.

As it is now, I think Federal regulations require a little paper stamp or something. Of course, that goes away the minute it gets off the boat. We couldn't get the muscle to pass that bill. And one of the reasons was, everybody was cheating. The big chains, the department store chains, the jewelry store chains, Natural Jewelers Association all came out against us on that bill, and we just couldn't get any traction on it. So we let it die. But it reinforced in my mind the need to do something.

Well, in 1990 when the bill was reintroduced, that was the first reintroduction, I think, since it was passed in the 1930s. It was clear that it needed to be addressed, because a lot of Indian people were being basically ripped off, by the things were being made in foreign countries.

And so we did introduce that bill. I might mention a couple of complications we had in testimony, which you may get to. No. 1 is defining who is Indian and who is not. It's easy to say, Well, if you're on a federally recognized roll, you must be Indian. But there are many Native Americans who are not.

I remember there was two Hopi cousins who testified in our hearing, which was here in Santa Fe in those years, John Kyle and I did it, Senator Kyle and I, and they were blood cousins. One was on the roll and one was not. Because the Hopi, like the Seneca and several other tribes, the blood line has

to come through the mother's side, not the father's side. And that creates a lot of ambiguity about who is—you know, how many are Indian or not.

And the other way for people to get enrolled is through lineal descendancy. And so the Cherokee and several other tribes—it doesn't make any difference how thin the blood gets. If you're one one-thousandth Native blood and the other 999 something else, under this Act, you qualify as Indian to make jewelry, if you're on that roll.

But that still left a lot of people off altogether. There are over 50 tribes right now trying to be reintroduced that were terminated in the 1950s. Some tribes, who are very big, like the Lumbee of the Carolinas, I think there's over 50,000 members. They are not a federally recognized tribe, but they are a State-recognized tribe. Creates another nuance about who is and who cannot make it.

But the most outlandish story I heard was of a Japanese citizen who arrived—I won't mention the tribe—but arrived at a Northern Plains Tribe with an interpreter about a year and a half ago, and he went to the Tribal headquarters. And through the interpreter, he told the people in the tribal office, "I'm a member of this tribe."

And of course, they said, "What?"

They didn't know what he was talking about. Well, he was. His father was in the military, stationed in Japan. He married a Japanese lady. They had a son. He put the son on the roll, and then they got a divorce. He came back to this country; she stayed in Japan.

And so the youngster was born and raised in Japan, only speaks Japanese, went to Japanese schools. Had to have an interpreter when he visited the American reservation. But under existing law, he could be sitting in downtown Tokyo making authentic Indian-made rings.

So kind of makes you scratch your head when somebody who is 50 percent can't get on a roll, but somebody who has never been in this country can be making authentic Indian jewelry.

There are many other cases like that. I just mention those as a couple of really extreme ones that we had to deal with.

But one of the other weaknesses, and I might mention the strengths of the bill that we passed in 1990, before that bill was passed, there was no legal, civil way you could go after somebody that was cheating and trying to say he was a Navajo if he wasn't. We put a section in that bill, as I remember, it authorized the tribe to sue up to something like $200,000 for misinterpreting your identity as being one of their tribal members when you are not.

And I think that section has been used a couple times, not against individuals, but against some of these big chains that are importing tons of so-called Indian jewelry. I think that's been enforced a couple times, and that's good. But the weakness of that section is—I'll give you an example.

If you drive from Flagstaff up to the Grand Canyon, you'll see many little booths on the side of the road. Little elderly ladies trying to sell a little necklace or something to get a loaf of bread for Sunday. Around Four Corners monument, it's the same. What if you go there, and you find out that lady—maybe she's very honest, "Oh, I got this from a trader."

So she doesn't know where it came from, except a trader. But if you have a good eye, you know by looking at it if it's authentic, if it's plastic beads, if it's machine-stamped, so on like that. What are you going to do about it? What if she is cheating? What if she even knows she's cheating? Think of the expense, the prosecutorial investigative expense of the Federal agencies to enforce that section of the law.

Nobody in their right mind is going to do that—at least not to my knowledge. They are not going to spend hundreds of thousands of dollars and all the stuff it takes to put some little old lady in jail, or fine her, because she's trying to make five bucks for a couple of loaves of bread. It just doesn't make sense. There's got to be some kind of an intermediate action that can be done that you can deal with that kind of a problem.

Yet one of the other weaknesses I saw of that bill that we passed was, some things that are made, more than one person works on them. So if a person—say you have five people, and they worked on a bracelet. And one guy designs it, the next guy frames it up, the next guy solders it, the next guy puts some stones in it. What if one of the five is Indian and the other four are not? How do you define that piece of jewelry? Is it Indian-made or is it not? I don't know, but it's something that I saw as a weakness.

I still judge. In fact, here in Santa Fe a couple years ago, my daughter and I, we judged contemporary jewelry. There's some very, very nice jewelry being turned out by some of our young people now. I'm an old timer; I learned how to do it all by hand. That's not the way things are done anymore. I mean, youngsters are very creative.

And so there was a very fine belt that we judged first place. I didn't know how it was made, but it was a very, very nice-looking belt. Well, I found out that belt was done, as many young artists do now, it was designed on a CAD/CAM.

So, okay, a Native person designed it on a CAD/CAM. The CAD/CAM was then—I don't remember if the word is "slated," "networked," or "integrated"—worked with a milling machine. And the milling machine cut out the pieces of jewelry. So you have to ask, "Well, okay, a Native person pushed a button. Does that make it Indian-made?"

Another person might say, "Well, yeah, wait a minute. He really didn't touch the thing. It was all made kind of automated." And I don't know the answer to that. Maybe you can figure that one out and deal with it in new legislation.

But these things keep arising. When I judged Santa Fe a couple years ago, I hadn't judged for a number of years before that. Now they have divisions for film, for clothing, design, all kinds of stuff that wasn't even in our realm of thinking in the old way of doing, Indian, quote/unquote, art. And I support that. It's given new avenues of expression for many of our Native youngsters, and I think that's great.

But it also makes it more important for a committee like this to ask, "How do you define who is what?"

And so with that, let me just check a couple of my own notes of anything that I did forget. Probably not. Those are the main things I kinda wanted to bring to the Committee to testify.

And with that, if you have any questions of me of what we did in the old days, I'd be glad to answer.

Senator UDALL. Senator Campbell, could you just say a word about prosecution? I know you picked the example of a lady trying to sell a bracelet. But if you have a big, like, some of these cases we've seen, international operations, you know, manufacturing, huge amounts of this stuff, representing it to be authentic Native American, bringing it over here from Philippines or China, wherever.

Senator CAMPBELL. And I have to say, Mr. Chairman, some of it's being sold right on the square here in Santa Fe. You know, being around it my whole life, I've got a pretty good eye about what is authentic and what is not. The Native people, when they make it themselves handmade, there's a weight and a heft and a design to it that you can almost qualify, once you've been around it most of your life as I have.

But once the money started coming in for Indian art, which is basically to say Indian jewelry in the late 1970s, we did see people from Japan, from China, from some of the Gulf countries, moving in literally, a number of them went out to the reservations themselves, to the pueblos, to Zuni and other tribes, and tried to tie up contracts with the craftsmen where they couldn't sell to anybody except them.

And that was not enough to have it done there. So then they actually started having it made overseas and importing it over into this country under the guise of being Indian-made. That is still going on. And the Mayor Becerra, I believe his name is, in Santa Fe, he's really taken the lead in trying to bring that to the forefront in the market here in Santa Fe.

But I think maybe one of the key things in this whole scene is, if you are an unsuspecting buyer, the best thing you can do is make sure you're dealing with somebody who can authenticate, and they can tell you exactly who made it and give you the address, if you want to go talk to them themself.

And if they can't do that, then you gotta say, "Well, I don't know where the heck that came from." Most of the people that I think that belong to, say, the Indian Arts and Crafts Board, Indian Arts and Crafts Association, they subscribe to a ethics—code of ethics, and I think they're pretty darn good in trying to represent exactly what it is.

But as I said, when you're going through four or five hands and four or five people working on it, I don't know. I still get pieces back, or I'll get parts of things, and somebody will come to me and say, "Ben, I've got this stone. I know it's really valuable because my grandmother owned it."

And I've just been around turquoise my whole darn life. And I look at it, and it looks like it's a piece of Coca-Cola bottle. And I don't want to hurt her feelings, so I don't even work on it. But I don't even want to tell her how bad the thing is, because I don't want to hurt her feelings, because a lot of people are just that un- aware about what authentic is, just what is real Indian turquoise.

By the way, for the uninitiated, one of easiest ways you can do it is with a hat pin or a needle. If you're unsure of the stone, and you heat that needle, like, red-hot and touch the stone, if nothing happens, that's real. But if a little bit of smoke comes up or a little smell like plastic, it ain't real. That's the layman's test how you can test to see if the turquoise is the real thing.

And if there's anything I can answer, Mr. Chairman, I will. But I commend you and Senator Heinrich on doing this hearing. It's well needed.

Senator UDALL. Well, thank you so much. We know you're busy on your trip down here and for taking a few minutes and sharing your thoughts and ideas with us. We hope you will think a little bit more about this and maybe submit written statements, as I'm going to tell everybody in the audience they have the ability to do, too.

So let's thank Senator Campbell.

Okay. We're going to start with our opening statements here, and then we'll go to the witnesses.

First of all, let me just welcome everybody to Indian Country and to thank everyone who made it out to Santa Fe. Some people, I think, traveled all the way from Washington, and so we really appreciate your being here. I very much look forward to today's discussion, exploring how to modernize the Indian Arts and Crafts

Act. It's long overdue, and I'm looking forward to a very productive day here.

Today's hearing is an official Senate committee hearing, the Senate Committee on Indian Affairs, and this is a field hearing what we're doing. The format today is the same as the format we use for hearings in Washington, D.C. The Committee will hear testimony from two panels of witnesses and Committee members will ask the witnesses questions.

I want to thank all the witnesses who have traveled here today to help us understand these issues, these very, very important issues to Indian Country, and figure out how we can do better to protect the cultural integrity of Native American arts and crafts. So today's Congressional hearing is not a town hall. I want to em- phasize that.

It's not a town hall, for example, where folks speak out from the audience and ask questions. We're here to take testi- mony, official testimony, with a court reporter, from our witnesses. However, we want to hear from everyone on this critical issue be- fore us. So you're invited and are most welcome to submit your comments and ideas. And to do that, you can e-mail them to *testimony@Indian.Senate.gov.*

That's *testimony@Indian.Senate.gov,* and my staff members are here with badges on, and so you can get that from them as you leave, too.

And Senator Heinrich's staff members are also here. We will leave the official record open for two weeks until July 21st, and I really encourage everyone to submit comments based on what you've heard here. And also, please feel free to talk to my staff, Senator Heinrich's staff, after this hearing with any questions. They're seated behind me. Many of these folks behind me are official Senate Indian Affairs staffers that have come out from Washington, and they're wearing staff ID badges. So you'll be able to identify them.

And then let me—first of all, I already thanked Roy Herrera, but I want to thank the Santa Fe Indian School again for hosting us, and Superintendent, for your very thoughtful opening remarks. Santa Fe Indian School is in good hands with Superintendent Herrera.

And I want to thank Jude for that beautiful opening prayer. You're one of the future leaders of Indian Country, and I'm glad you're here to witness the legislative process in action. We sometimes call that in the Senate, and Senator Campbell calls it sausage-making.

But the Santa Fe Indian School was established in 1890 to educate Native American youth from tribes throughout the Southwest. It was established during the boarding-school era, a shameful period when the Federal government removed Native children from their communities and attempted to assimilate them into Anglo society; among other things, prohibiting children from speaking their Native languages and practicing their beliefs.

Sitting here today on the grounds of this tribally controlled school located on pueblo land, it's clear to see—and I'm proud to say—that our nation has made great strides from its disastrous policies of the past. Santa Fe Indian School and other Native American—other Native schools exercise educational sovereignty by promoting Native languages and affirming cultural identity by supporting Native students' cultural and traditional beliefs.

But we still need to do much more to protect cultural sovereignty and do that for now and for the future. That's why I chose Santa Fe Indian School as the location for this hearing, to highlight the gains we've made and the work that still needs to be done.

As the Vice Chair of the Senate Committee on Indian Affairs, I intend to hold a series of hearings right here in New Mexico that focus on supporting cultural identity to make sure future generations of Native Americans have what elders have; pride in Native American culture and a way to practice time-honored traditions of craftsmanship while maintaining a livelihood.

We've got a serious problem on our hands as we heard from Senator Campbell. Imitation Indian arts and crafts flooding the market in places like Gallup and Albuquerque, Phoenix, and right here in Santa Fe.

A network of swindlers are making millions of dollars off the backs of Native Americans. This situation is wholly unacceptable. The mass production of imitation Native American jewelry and other crafts destabilizes the Indian art market, forcing Native American artisans to drop prices to keep up with wholesale prices of so-called Native American jewelry that is actually fake. Artificially low prices then force Native Americans to quit their crafts, crafts that often have been passed down over many generations.

Arts and crafts are a major economic driver for Indian Country. Fake art drives down prices, forces Native Americans to quit their crafts and devalues Native American art. We want this to stop. We want to see Native Americans reap the well-earned benefits of their art.

Santa Fe is at the epicenter of the problem. Our city is driven by tourism, and many tourists come here to experience Native American culture and to buy Native American arts and crafts. But many unknowingly buy imitation products, fueling the black market, yet we have hardly talked about this problem.

So this hearing is important for a number of reasons. Most importantly, to ensure that the cultural integrity of authentic Indian arts and crafts, and by looking for ways to improve enforcement of the Indian Arts and Crafts Act. We need to do more to address this problem.

I'm encouraged by the recent efforts of the U.S. Fish and Wildlife Service and the U.S. Attorneys' Office. For example, in the last couple of years, the U.S. Attorneys' Office charged three New Mexicans with violating the Indian Arts and Crafts Act by importing and fraudulently selling foreign-made jewelry as Native American-made. That was an international scheme that you've heard a little bit about already.

And in February of this year, the U.S. Attorneys' Office indicted several more people, including one person from the earlier case, with violating the Act for the same types of crimes.

Appropriation of Native American art is not a new issue. This has been happening for decades. As Attorney General in 1996, I sued these scammers for violating the State's Unfair Businesses Practice Act.

So during today's hearing, we will explore how to improve enforcement efforts. Another goal of this hearing is to build consumer awareness of the problem so the consumers can make informed decisions in buying Native American arts and crafts. The fact is, consumers want to purchase goods that are authentic.

So again, thank you to all the witnesses for being here today, and now I'd like to turn to my good friend and colleague, Senator Heinrich, for his opening remarks. Senator Heinrich has been a very strong advocate for Native Americans. He has several pieces of legislation that he's already passed in his Congressional career, and I look forward to continuing to work with him on the very important issues that will be outlined today.

Senator Heinrich.

STATEMENT OF HON. MARTIN HEINRICH, U.S. SENATOR FROM NEW MEXICO

Senator HEINRICH. Thank you, Mr. Vice Chairman. And I want to start as well by thanking as well the Santa Fe Indian School for hosting us today. And I really want to thank Senator Udall for shining a light on this issue. We are very lucky to have him as the vice chair of this Committee. And this new look at what we can do to update this law is incredibly important.

I want to welcome and thank Senator Ben Nighthorse Campbell who worked on this bill back in the day. It's really important that we hear from people who have your level of expertise. So I very much appreciate you being here today. And I want to thank the Senate Indian Affairs Committee staff for all of their hard work in putting this together.

Welcome to our panelists. We have an incredible panel of folks to offer testimony here today. And I want to take just a moment and thank the Santa Fe Police Department and the BIA law enforcement officers who are with us here today.

In New Mexico, we all recognize the incredible beauty and worth of American Indian art. From the art left long ago on canyon walls in places like Chaco Canyon, and the Gila cliff dwellings, to traditional and modern art masterpieces created by Native American artists to this day.

Here in Santa Fe, some of our nation's leading Native artists are trained in the Santa Fe Indian School and at the Institute of American Arts. And more than a thousand Native artists gather here every August to display and sell their art at the annual Santa Fe Indian Market. The sale of Native American art and craftwork is a tremendous economic driver for tribal communities in our state and throughout Indian Country and the West.

New Mexicans understand the value of supporting true tribal artists and recognize the dangers posed by counterfeit items or items claiming to be Native-produced. For centuries, the United States used cultural appropriation as a tool of colonization. Today when non-Indians sell jewelry or pottery as Indian art, they are denying the right of tribal communities to define and control what tribal art is. This cultural appropriation removes Native art in traditions from their rightful context and denies the right of tribal communities to maintain sovereignty over their history and their culture.

When tribal communities are denied ownership of their own cultures, they lose the ability to maintain their language, their beliefs; literally, their way of life. The Indian Arts and Crafts Act of 1990 is essentially a truth-in-advertising law that prohibits misrepresentation or falsely displaying arts or crafts as Indian-produced.

We're here today to learn more about whether the law is working and what steps we need to take to make sure that all products marketed are marketed truthfully so that Native artists can thrive in an ethical marketplace.

I would also like to quickly touch on another important issue in New Mexico, which I've been proud to work with Senator Udall and the tribes across New Mexico with. Many tribes in New Mexico have experienced people literally stealing and trafficking objects that are not art but are essential religious and cultural patrimony. When someone steals and sells a tribe's cultural patrimony, they are stealing that tribe's traditions and identity.

Last month I was proud to reintroduce the bipartisan Safeguard Tribal Objects and Patrimony or STOP Act, a bill to prohibit export of sacred Native American items. And that increases penalties for stealing and illegally trafficking tribal cultural patrimony.

I announced the bill's reintroduction during a meeting with the students from the Santa Fe Indian School Leadership Institute Summer Policy Academy in my office in Washington. And I was incredibly moved by the unique perspectives and personal stories that those students offered. They talked a lot about the responsibility that they felt to preserve their cultural heritage and fulfill their sacred trust as generations before them have.

That's what's at the heart of today's hearing for me. And with that, I want to thank all of you again, and I look forward to hearing from our two panels.

Senator UDALL. Thank you, Senator Heinrich so much, and thank you for your good, hard work on the STOP Act, which is for the protection of cultural patrimony.

We will now hear from our first panel. Mr. William Woody, Chief of Law Enforcement at the U.S. Fish and Wildlife Service, a bureau of the Department of Interior. Miss Meredith Stanton, Director of the Indian Arts and Crafts Board, an agency of the U.S. Department of Interior, and Miss Gretchen Shappert, Assistant Director, Executive Office of the U.S. Attorneys at the U.S. Department of Justice.

I want to remind the witnesses that your full written testimony will be made a part of the official hearing record. Please keep your statements to five minutes so that we may have time for questions. And I look forward to hearing your testimony, beginning with Miss Stanton.

Thank you very much and please proceed.

STATEMENT OF MEREDITH STANTON, DIRECTOR, INDIAN ARTS AND CRAFTS BOARD, U.S. DEPARTMENT OF THE INTERIOR

Ms. STANTON. Thank you. Good morning, Vice Chairman Udall and Senator Heinrich. I would like to also start the testimony here today by thanking Chairman Hoeven for holding this hearing.

I am Meredith Stanton, Director of the Indian Arts and Crafts Board. I've worked for the Board for almost 40 years and have been an enrolled member of the Delaware Nation of Oklahoma. I appreciate this opportunity to testify before you today about the Board. I work to promote and protect authentic Indian art, artists, and the Indian Arts and Crafts Act.

The Board was established by Congress in 1935 and operates with an annual budget of approximately 1.4 million, a staff of nine employees, and one detailee stationed here in New Mexico. The Board is the only Federal agency that is exclusively concerned with the economic benefits of Indian cultural development. Sales of Indian art exceed a billion dollars each year.

With the very broad economic development and cultural preservation mission, we operate three museums; one in South Dakota, one in Montana, and one in Oklahoma to promote emerging Indian artists. Marketing seminars and publications are important components of our services.

For example, our new brochure promotes authentic Navajo weaving to help offset the weavers' stiff competition from counterfeit Navajo rugs. The arts are at the very heart of our ancestral and contemporary Indian society and culture. The New Mexico, and throughout the Southwest, Indian art production and sales are critically important to the economic stability and viability of Indian artists, communities, and tribes.

In response to the growing sales of counterfeit Indian products, Congress passed the Indian Arts and Crafts Act of 1990. A top priority of the Board, the Act is a truth-in-marketing law to combat the sale of counterfeit Indian art and to protect the Indian artists' economic livelihood. The Act prohibits the marketing of art as Indian-made if it is not made by an Indian as defined by the Act.

Each day Indian economic livelihoods are eroded by the fierce competition of lower-priced, imported counterfeit Indian products. High-priced knockoffs of one-of-a-kind master Indian jewelry also contribute to the erosion of consumer confidence in the Indian art market nationwide.

To help remedy the problem, the Board promotes authentic Indian art and art protections through participation in events, including the Santa Fe Indian Market, and consumer education, such as our collaborations with the New Mexico Attorney General's Office in a brochure promoting authentic New Mexico Indian art. The Board distributes this brochure at the Sunport, visitors' centers, and Indian art businesses and markets throughout the state.

The Act designated the FBI to investigate Act cases. However, the Indian Arts and Crafts Enforcement Act of 2010, which then Senator Heinrich was a cosponsor, allows now all Federal law enforcement officers to conduct Act investigations. This led to the 2012 agreement between the Board and the U.S. Fish and Wildlife Service.

Since then, the scope and depth of Act investigations have increased exponentially. While complaints and violations have often occurred primarily in the Southwest and particularly here in New Mexico, the scope of the problem is nationwide.

Since 1996, the Board has received over 1700 complaints of alleged Act violations, of which 1300 have been addressed to date.

We have been—we've had 22 Federal prosecutions in New Mexico, Alaska, Utah, Michigan, South Dakota, and Missouri.

The Board has also worked with the Office of the State Attorney General here in New Mexico on six cases involving the misrepresentation of Indian art. Our sweeping Service Act investigation to date involves a large-scale conspiracy to import and fraudulently sell Filipino-made jewelry as Indian-made.

Chief Woody will discuss that further in his testimony.

The Act has its challenges, and a tremendous amount of work remains to dismantle these counterfeit Indian art networks, certainly in New Mexico and nationwide. These counterfeits hinder the passing down from one generation to the next of important Indian traditions, skills, and heritage—true American treasures.

The Department is committed to protecting Indian artists from counterfeits and looks forward to working with our Congressional colleagues to ensure the goals of the Act are met.

Thank you, Senators Udall and Heinrich, for your interest in supporting and protecting these true American treasures.

[The prepared statement of Ms. Stanton follows:]

PREPARED STATEMENT OF MEREDITH STANTON, DIRECTOR, INDIAN ARTS AND CRAFTS BOARD, U.S. DEPARTMENT OF THE INTERIOR

Introduction

Good Morning Vice Chairman Udall and Senator Heinrich. I am Meridith Stanton, Director of the Indian Arts and Crafts Board, within the Department of the Interior, which I have served for almost 40 years. I am also an enrolled member of the Delaware Nation of Oklahoma. I appreciate this opportunity to testify before you today about the Indian Arts and Crafts Board, our work to promote and protect authentic American and Indian artists, artisans, and their creative work, and the Indian Arts and Crafts Act of 1990 (Public Law 101–644), as amended.

The Indian Arts and Crafts Board (Board) was created by Congress in 1935 to promote American Indian and Alaska Native economic development through the expansion of the Indian arts and crafts market. The Board is the only Federal agency that is consistently and exclusively concerned with economic benefits of Native American cultural development. We have a current staff of nine full-time employees and one detailee who is stationed in New Mexico. The Board's policies are determined by the Board of Commissioners, who are appointed by the Secretary of the Interior and serve without compensation. The Board has a very broad economic development and cultural preservation mission, and operates three Indian museums in South Dakota, Montana, and Oklahoma. The museum programs include special exhibitions to promote emerging Indian artists, Indian Youth Art Competitions and art classes to encourage the development of future Indian master artists, and cultural programming to educate consumers about the inherent value of authentic Indian art.

Business development, marketing, and Intellectual Property Rights Protection workshops, seminars, and publications for Indian artists, businesses, and consumers are also important components of the Board's services. For example, the Board and New Mexico State Attorney General's office collaborated on a brochure to promote New Mexico Indian art. This brochure is distributed at the Board's consumer education booth at each annual Santa Fe Indian Market, at the Albuquerque airport visitor kiosk, New Mexico visitor centers, and Indian art businesses and markets throughout the State. The Board also recently prepared a brochure it will distribute nationwide to promote authentic Navajo weaving and to help offset the challenges weavers are facing due to competition from Navajo style and counterfeit Navajo weavings.

The Indian Arts and Crafts Act

In response to growing sales of counterfeit Indian products in the billion-dollar Indian art market, Congress passed the Indian Arts and Crafts Act of 1990. The Act is a truth-in-advertising law that authorized the Board to refer complaints of counterfeit Indian Goods to the Federal Bureau of Investigation (FBI). It provides criminal and civil penalties for marketing products as "Indian made" when such products are not made by Indians, as defined by the Act. Under the Act, work marketed as authentic Indian art and craftwork must be produced by an artist or artisan who is an enrolled member of a federally or officially State recognized Indian tribe, or an Indian Artisan certified by the tribe of their direct descent.

Implementing and enforcing the Act is a top priority for the Board. Enforcement of the Act protects Native American artists and craftspeople, businesses, and Tribes, as well as consumers. It also protects the integrity of Native American cultural heritage and the economic self-reliance of Tribes and their members. The Act provides critical economic benefits for Native American cultural development by recognizing that forgery and fraudulent Indian arts and crafts diminish the livelihood of Native American artists and craftspeople by lowering both market prices and standards.

Scope of the Problem

In 2011, a Government Accountability Act report [1] found that "The sale of goods falsely represented as authentic Indian-produced arts and crafts has been a persistent and potentially growing problem in the United States." It continued that "Misrepresentation by sale of unauthentic products created by non-Indians, including imports from foreign countries, is a matter of great concern to Indian artists, who have to reduce their prices or lose sales because of competition from lower priced imitation products."

While complaints and violations have often occurred primarily in the Southwest, particularly in New Mexico, due to the Indian art industry's concentration in this region, the scope of the problem is nationwide. Since 1996, the Board has received over 1,700 complaints of alleged Act violations, of which 1,295 have been closed and 413 remain open investigations. Many of these were handled administratively, through letters informing businesses and individuals about the Act and Act compliance. Others were referred for investigation to federal, and at times State, law enforcement authorities, depending on the nature of the complaint and jurisdiction. To date, there have been 22 federal prosecutions in New Mexico, Alaska, Utah, South Dakota, and Missouri. The Board has also worked with the Office of the New Mexico Attorney General on five cases involving the misrepresentation of Indian art.

Working with Our Partners

The Indian Arts and Crafts Enforcement Act of 2010 authorized all federal law enforcement officers, not just the FBI, to conduct investigations and revised the Act's criminal penalties. Following passage of this legislation, in 2012 the Board entered into a memorandum of agreement and reimbursable support agreement with the U.S. Fish and Wildlife Service (Service) for law enforcement agents to work Act cases.

In the years leading up to the agreement with the Service, the Board collected evidence of fraudulent activity in the Southwest. That advance work was followed by an extensive investigation led by the Service, Operation Al Zuni, the most sweeping and successful investigation and enforcement of the Act to date.

The Board works with many tribes, state and local agencies and federal partners to enforce the Act. These collaborations significantly strengthen the Board's ability to successfully address counterfeit Indian art and craftwork. The Board has successfully worked cases and taken other actions to remedy violations of the law, such as those involving the fraudulent marketing of rugs as Navajo, jewelry as Hopi, jewelry as Apache, and art as Cherokee, as well as a settlement with Pendleton Woolen Mills regarding their use of Indian names to market non-Indian products.

Conclusion

For the highly talented, dedicated, and hard-working Indian artists and artisans, Indian art is more than an income producing activity. Traditional Indian art and craftwork, and evolving and cutting edge Indian art, respectively, are at the very heart of Indian ancestral and contemporary society and culture.

There are challenges to achieving the goals of the Act and there remains a tremendous amount of work to dismantle these counterfeit Indian art networks certainly in New Mexico, and nationwide. The Board will continue to pursue robust Act enforcement in partnership with the Service. We are committed to protecting Indian artists from competition with counterfeit Indian art, which hinders the passing down from one generation to the next of important Indian traditions, heritage, and skills—true American treasures. The Department looks forward to working with our

---

[1] INDIAN ARTS AND CRAFTS: Size of Market and Extent of Misrepresentation Are Unknown GAO–11–432: Published: Apr 28, 2011. Publicly Released: Apr 28, 2011. *http:// www.gao.gov/products/GAO-11-432*

Congressional colleagues to ensure the goals of the Act are met and to preserve the cultures, heritages and self-determination of tribes and Alaska Native communities.
Thank you, Senators Udall and Heinrich, for your interest in supporting and protecting Indian artists and Indian economies through the creative arts. I am pleased to answer any questions you may have.

Senator UDALL. Miss Stanton, thank you so much for your testimony.
And Chief Woody, please proceed.

STATEMENT OF WILLIAM WOODY, CHIEF, OFFICE OF LAW ENFORCEMENT, U.S. FISH AND WILDLIFE SERVICE, U.S. DEPARTMENT OF THE INTERIOR

Mr. WOODY. Good afternoon, Vice Chairman Udall and Senator Heinrich. I want to start by thanking you and Chairman Hoeven for holding this hearing in support.

I am William Woody. I'm Chief of Law Enforcement for the U.S. Fish and Wildlife Service in the Department of Interior. And I appreciate the opportunity to testify before you today regarding our collaborative work with the Indian Arts and Crafts Board to enforce the Indian Arts and Crafts Act.

The protection of tribal nations is of the utmost importance to the Department of Interior in safeguarding tribal arts and crafts integral to that mission and vital to the economic livelihoods and culture of tribal nations. The sale of Native American arts and crafts by individual producers, businesses, tribal-run operations, and other members of overall Native Americans, as Meredith states, is over a billion dollars a year.

Criminal investigations, both nationally and internationally and to individuals and businesses making fraudulent Native American arts and crafts, and the sale or offer for sale of those counterfeit items in the United States are complex, requiring technical expertise, significant long-term investigative capability, and an international presence.

Since 2012, the services maintained the memorandum of agreement with the Board to serve as the enforcement arm of the department to lead criminal investigations and allegations of violations of the Act. Given cases our agents have been working on and additional information we have received from the last several years, it is fair to say the scope of the problem is far larger than expected. Investigative activity thus far has been extensive and far-reaching, taking place not only here in New Mexico, Arizona, and Texas, California and Colorado, Alaska, Nevada, Hawaii.

I have a few slides I'd like to show you to illustrate the extent and complexity of the issue. But I think you need to understand one thing. Being able to prove many of these cases is very complex, and getting a conviction beyond a reasonable doubt is—it isn't based on just hunches or assumptions, too.

So Operation Al Zuni involves fraudulent Native American jewelry sales under the Act. During the course of this operation, we uncovered two organized networks who had been a Native American jewelry business for years and who perpetuated an international scheme to illegally sell Filipino-made jewelry as authentic Native American-made in the U.S.

Agents were able to access these manufacturing facilities in the Philippines, document and track shipments of counterfeit jewelry as they made their way to the U.S., and then traced them to retail locations where they were being sold as authentic Native American-made.

First slide.

This surveillance photo shows a shipment of fraudulent jewelry from the Philippines. Prior to this photo being taken, there was a significant amount of work done to ID the source and track the shipment to where this UPS driver is delivering it.

Slide two, please.

This shipment was tracked by our agents to a UPS hub, detained, opened, and inspected, and allowed to continue to its destination.

Third slide, please. This shows some of the jewelry from just one of those boxes. So it is counterfeit jewelry from one of the boxes. There are—if you look at these bags there's 50 to 100 items, whether they be rings, necklaces, pendants, bracelets, mass produced.

Slide four, please.

This is a more detailed photo of the items in the shipment. The photo on the left shows an original Native American-made pendant that was sent to the Philippines to be reproduced. The image on the right is one of the replicas that was found in the intercepted shipment. They look nearly identical. If you'll note the one on the right, look at the price tag up in the corner of that particular items. You've got a $90 price tag on that.

I think that particular item is being made pennies on the dollar, if you will. So that's really—I mean, if you picture—I guess the best term I would give it is, these factories that we see, it's pretty much like a sweat shop. Which you look at is, there's 40 to 50 people in the shop—and I'll just use this as an example.

They have this sitting in front of them, and they're making this particular same item, just mass-produced. So if you opened one of those bags previously, what you end up seeing is all the same item. And the only way to get this, as I stated, these are very complex investigations. Following that all the way from the beginning, in this case, the Philippines, all the way to the sale, is complex and takes a long time.

Slide five, please.

This counterfeit ring was intercepted and marked prior to the delivery of the shipment to a retail location.

Slide six. This is really the last step in the process. Our agents purchased this ring and other counterfeit jewelry being sold by a retailer, labeled as authentic Native American-made by a particular artist.

Slide seven.

Slide seven—while she's working on that, we ultimately executed 16 search warrants and seized over 200,000 pieces of jewelry, much of it as shown in the photo, which is not coming up.

Counterfeit jewelry that was imported in this case by the business has an approximate declared value of $11 million. That was their declared direct value of the importers bringing it in.

However, the prices that they would receive for these items when they were sold as authentic Native American, either wholesale or retail, is substantially higher. To date, six of the subjects in this case have been indicted and are awaiting trial. In addition to charges of violating the Act, Federal prosecutors have also charged the defendants with violations, Federal fraudulent importation, money laundering, wire fraud, and mail fraud.

The service is committed to continuing this important work in partnership with all Federal, state, tribal, and county offices, and the Board, and looks forward to working with you to raise awareness on this issue and improve implementation of the Indian Arts and Crafts Board.

If you look at in this slide that just comes up, think about this, all of those boxes, everything you see in there, is just from one case. As I stated, just talking with the agents—and I had a chance to talk to them yesterday on some of the projects they're working on—this is one. There's many more.

It is, as Mr. Ben Nighthorse Campbell talked about, the folks on the roadside, what you've got is, you've got some significant stuff still coming into this country that needs to be dealt with.

And again, we are committed to this important work, and we look forward to working with all the agencies and senators. I want to thank you for the opportunity to testify today, and I look forward to taking your questions. Thank you.

[The prepared statement of Mr. Woody follows:]

PREPARED STATEMENT OF WILLIAM WOODY, CHIEF, OFFICE OF LAW ENFORCEMENT, U.S. FISH AND WILDLIFE SERVICE, U.S. DEPARTMENT OF THE INTERIOR

Introduction

Good afternoon Vice Chairman Udall and Senator Heinrich. I am William Woody, Chief of the Office of Law Enforcement for the U.S. Fish and Wildlife Service (Service), in the Department of the Interior. I appreciate the opportunity to testify before you today on our work to enforce the Indian Arts and Crafts Act (Act) and address fraudulent Native American art and crafts in the United States.

The Office of Law Enforcement's primary responsibility is to focus on significant threats to wildlife resources—illegal trade, unlawful commercial exploitation, habitat destruction, and environmental hazards. The Office of Law Enforcement investigates wildlife crimes; regulates wildlife trade; helps Americans understand and comply with wildlife protection laws; and works in partnership with international, Federal, State, and tribal counterparts to conserve wildlife resources.

The Service's Office of Law Enforcement has a workforce comprised of special agents, conservation law enforcement officers, and wildlife inspectors stationed at ports of entry, regional locations, and field offices across the country, as well as attachés stationed at various embassies around the world. When fully staffed, we have 140 wildlife inspectors and 261 special agents. Our wildlife inspectors work at major ports of entry across the nation to facilitate legal trade in wildlife and wildlife products and check inbound and outbound shipments for illegal wildlife and wildlife products. Service inspectors also utilize seven canine detector dogs to facilitate cargo searches for illegal wildlife and wildlife products. Our special agents conduct complex investigations to detect and document international illegal wildlife trafficking, unlawful destruction and harm of endangered species and other trust species such as migratory birds, and crimes involving the unlawful exploitation of native and foreign species in interstate commerce. Our International Attaché program places special agents in U.S. embassies to investigate international wildlife trafficking, share and coordinate intelligence, expand training programs, provide technical assistance, and work collaboratively with partners in the regions they are stationed. Attaché locations include: Bangkok, Thailand; Dar es Salaam, Tanzania; Gaborone, Botswana; Lima, Peru; Beijing, China; and Libreville, Gabon.

With this technical expertise, investigative capability, and international presence, the Service is uniquely suited within the Department of Interior to enforce the Act. The protection of tribal nations is of the utmost importance to the Department, and safeguarding tribal art and crafts is integral to that mission and vital to the livelihoods and culture of tribal nations. The Service is committed to fulfilling this role on behalf of the Department and in partnership with the Indian Arts and Crafts Board (Board).

Since 2012, the Service has maintained a Memoranda of Agreement with the Board to serve as the enforcement arm of the Department and lead criminal investigations into alleged violations of the Act. The Board provides funding to the Service to cover the salaries of assigned agents, their travel, supplies, equipment, and other needs. These agents are specifically assigned to work cases related to the Act and have led our investigations to date.

Operation Al Zuni

Operation Al Zuni is a multi-year investigation that centered around two organized networks who have been in the Native American jewelry business for years, and who perpetrated an international scheme to illegally sell Filipino-made jewelry as authentic Native-American-made. Through our investigations, we learned that members of both networks established and operated manufacturing facilities in the Philippines for the purpose of replicating and producing Native American-style jewelry and crafts. The items were then exported to business associates in the United States and sold in stores in Albuquerque, Gallup, Santa Fe, and Zuni, NM, and Calistoga, CA as genuine Native American items. The businesses imported Native American-style jewelry with an approximate declared value of $11 million. However, the networks were able to turn a large profit at the retail level on these items, as the value of this jewelry sold as authentic Native American-made items is substantially higher.

Operation Al Zuni is the largest investigation to date into fraudulent Native American jewelry sales under the Act. Over a period of four years, special agents based in the Southwest built the case by collaborating with the Federal Bureau of Investigation (FBI), Homeland Security Investigations (HSI), and our own attaché in Bangkok to visit the manufacturing facilities in the Philippines. Wildlife inspectors and special agents would document and mark the fraudulent jewelry, track the shipment to the final destination in the U.S., and follow it to its distribution and ultimate display in retail locations in New Mexico and California. Our agents were also able to purchase marked fraudulent items through undercover purchases. The Service partnered with numerous state, federal, and foreign agencies throughout the investigation, including on the day of the execution of the search warrants and arrest warrants, when we worked closely with the FBI, HSI, U.S. Marshals Service, Drug Enforcement Administration (DEA), the Bureau of Indian Affairs, New Mexico Department of Game and Fish, California Department of Fish and Wildlife, tribal law enforcement authorities, and the Philippine National Bureau of Investigations.

The investigative activity has been extensive and far-reaching, taking place in New Mexico, Arizona, Texas, California, Colorado, Alaska, Nevada and the Philippines.

Our work led to the execution of sixteen search warrants and three arrest warrants with the seizure of approximately $320,000 in funds, over 200,000 pieces of jewelry, and one vehicle. To date, six of the subjects have been indicted, pending trial. In addition to charges of violating the Act, federal prosecutors have also charged the defendants with violations of federal fraudulent importation, money laundering, wire fraud and mail fraud laws. Through the course of this investigation, other businesses and individuals have been identified but not yet charged.

Those charged to date include Imad Aysheh, formerly of Gallup, NM, and Iyad Aysheh, of Lodi, CA. Imad is the owner and operator of Imad's Jewelry, a jewelry manufacturing business in the Philippines. Iyad is CEO and agent for IJ Wholesale, Inc., a California corporation that imports jewelry into the United States. The Aysheh family built the international scheme, established the production facilities, sent authentic Native American items to the Philippines to be mass reproduced, and then imported the fraudulent pieces into the U.S. for illegal sale.

Also charged were Nael Ali and Mohammad Abed Manasra, both of Albuquerque, NM; Nedal Aysheh, formerly of Gallup, NM; and Raed Aysheh, of American Canyon, CA. Ali is the owner of two jewelry stores, Gallery 8 and Galleria Azul, in Albuquerque's Old Town that purport to specialize in the sale of Native American jewelry. Manasra is a wholesaler of Native American jewelry, and Raed and Nedal are partners managing Golden Bear & Legacy, LLC, a retail store in Calistoga, CA that specializes in Native American-style jewelry. These individuals distributed and sold the jewelry that was made in the Philippines and transported to the U.S. by the Aysheh family.

As a result of the actions taken in this investigation, numerous business and networks identified throughout this case have either discontinued the production and importation of fraudulent Native American jewelry, or changed their business practices to include properly labeling items with the country of origin.

Scope of the Problem

Despite the successful results of Operation Al Zuni, we believe we have just scratched the surface of the illegal activity occurring in the southwestern United States, and across the country. As evidenced by the 2011 Indian Arts and Crafts GAO report, there is much more that can be done to enforce the Act. In addition, our investigative work has shown that there is a significant presence of fraudulent Native American jewelry for sale in retail stores in the four-corners region of the Southwest. This influx of fraudulent jewelry drives legitimate Native American artists out of a flooded market and in some cases forces them to cooperate with the distributors in order to maintain a livelihood. Further, our investigation has only examined markets for fraudulent jewelry. We have not begun to take a comprehensive look into the markets for other Native American items in the Southwest, including pottery, paintings, blankets, etc., where there is likely similar fraudulent activity that is occurring.

Furthermore, we believe this is not just a problem for the markets in the Southwest. Other locations across the country that have high volume sales for tourists and visitors are prime targets for illegal activity to sell fraudulent Native American art and crafts. We have seen evidence to that effect. The Service has built cases in Alaska and Hawaii, with very similar circumstances involving areas with high tourist sales, but involving different types of art. They help exemplify and illustrate the potential scope and geographic reach of this illegal activity.

In southeast Alaska, the Service began an investigation in May 2014 based on complaints from tourists regarding the illegal misrepresentation of bone art carvings as genuine Alaska Native products. Our investigation found that the products were actually made by local non-native carvers and were being fraudulently labeled as genuine Alaska Native products. Charges were filed against four business owners and one employee for violations of the Act. These resulted in four convictions, thou- sands of dollars in fines and restitution, and twelve years of combined probation. In Hawaii, our investigations took a slightly different turn in that we found fraud- ulent Native American art and crafts being made with illegal wildlife products. As part of a joint undercover investigation with the National Oceanic and Atmospheric Administration from 2013 to 2015, the Service uncovered a smuggling ring in Hono- lulu run through Hawaiian Accessories, Inc. The company was found to be selling illegally acquired ivory, bone, and coral carvings and jewelry made from whale, wal- rus, black coral and other wildlife. The illegal wildlife products were sent to the Philippines to be carved and then smuggled back to Hawaii to be sold and fraudu- lently labeled as genuine Hawaiian-made products. As a result of our investigation, the president of Hawaiian Accessories, Inc. and several employees were sentenced for felony charges of conspiracy, smuggling wildlife into and out of the U.S., and violations of the Lacey Act.

Another area of concern uncovered by our investigations is individual, high profile artists utilizing false tribal affiliations. These artists promote a fraudulent cultural standing within the Native art community and take lucrative art show slots away from legitimate Native artists. For example, in response to a complaint to the Board, the Service investigated an individual for utilizing a fraudulent tribal identification card to sell his Indian artwork at fairs and on-line. Our investigation, which included an undercover buy, confirmed that Terry Lee Whetstone, of Odessa, MO was using a fraudulent Cherokee Nation of Oklahoma enrollment card in conjunction with the sale of his products. The Cherokee Nation verified that Terry Lee Whetstone is not a citizen of the Cherokee Nation. Whetstone pled guilty and was sentenced to three years of probation in 2015.

Conclusion

Investigations conducted by Service special agents, specifically Operation Al Zuni, have been very successful in enforcing the Indian Arts and Crafts Act and finally bringing criminals who have illegally sold fraudulent Native American art for years to justice. However, the scope of the problem is far larger than expected. The U.S. Fish and Wildlife Service has established a strong partnership with the Indian Arts and Crafts Board to enforce the Act, educate consumers about the issue of fraudulent art, and deter further illegal activity. The protection of tribal nations is of the utmost importance to the Department of the Interior, and safeguarding tribal art and crafts is integral to that mission and vital to the livelihoods and culture of tribal nations. The Service is committed to continuing this important work and looks forward to working with you to raise awareness of the issue and improve implementation of the Indian Arts and Crafts Act.

Senator UDALL. Thank you, Chief Woody.

Please, Miss Shappert, please go forward.

STATEMENT OF GRETCHEN C.F. SHAPPERT, ASSISTANT DIRECTOR, INDIAN, VIOLENT AND CYBER CRIME, EXECUTIVE OFFICE OF U.S. ATTORNEYS, U.S. DEPARTMENT OF JUSTICE

Ms. SHAPPERT. Thank you. My name is Gretchen Shappert. I'm the Assistant Director for the Indian, Violent and Cyber Crime Staff for the Department of Justice. I want to thank the Vice Chairman and Senator Heinrich for this opportunity and for documenting this very important field hearing. I also want to thank the Santa Fe Indian School for this opportunity.

The Indian Arts and Crafts Act was enacted to protect Native American artists and artisans who rely on the creation and sale of traditional and contemporary art and craftwork to support their economic livelihood, preserve their unique heritage, and transfer their extraordinary culture and values to succeeding generations. Under the Act, it is illegal to sell art or craft products in a manner that falsely suggests those products were produced by American Indians and Alaska Natives.

A 2011 Government Accountability Office Report concluded that the size of the Indian arts and crafts markets and the extent of misrepresentation are unknown, in part because no national database specifically tracks Indian arts and craft sales or misrepresentations. Furthermore, the GOA Report noted that U.S. Federal and state laws protecting intellectual property rights do not explicitly include Native American and Alaska Native traditional knowledge and cultural expressions—such as the processes for weaving baskets—and therefore provide little protection for them.

Native American artisans have voiced concerns that the traditional knowledge of how to create Native arts and crafts—often passed down from generation to generation within the tribes—will not be carried forward by younger generations if they cannot make a living producing these goods. Hence, enforcement and education about the current Act is vital to ensuring the integrity of Native arts and crafts.

Here in the District of New Mexico, my colleagues in the U.S. Attorneys' Office have used the criminal provisions of the Act, together with other Federal statutes, to prosecute criminal misrepresentations of inauthentic items as genuine Indian arts and crafts. Two criminal prosecutions will demonstrate the significance of these cases.

Andrew Gene Alvarez of Woffard Heights, California, was a prominent jeweler who alternately represented himself as Mescalero Apache, Colville, and Mayo Indian. He also used an alias, "Andrew Red Horse Alvarez." He came to the attention of Federal law enforcement because he was misrepresenting jewelry that he was selling in an art show at the Santa Fe Convention Center and said it was made by an Indian. Mr. Alvarez was prosecuted under the Act here in New Mexico, entered a guilty plea and was sentenced to 30 months of probation to be followed by a year of supervised release.

As part of his sentence, he was prohibited from representing that any of the jewelry he produced was of Indian origin. According to

Federal law enforcement officials in New Mexico, this prosecution was widely noted in the Native arts and crafts market, thereby serving as a potential deterrent to other potential fraudsters who might be tempted to engage in similar conduct.

The second example of criminal prosecution here in New Mexico was a case of Rose Morris—she was on one of the slides we saw earlier—who was sentenced to a probationary sentence of five years—and excuse me—of a prosecution payment of $38,000, having claimed the rugs she was selling were made by Native Americans. In fact, she randomly purchased the rugs from miscellaneous sources with no connection to Native craftsmen.

In other cases, Federal prosecutors have used a wide variety of Federal statutes—wire fraud and mail fraud in particular—to apprehend criminal offenders engaged in similar fraudulent conduct involving misrepresentation of supposedly Indian arts and crafts.

Criminal prosecutions are not the only way that Federal prosecutors support enforcement of the Indian Arts and Crafts Act. Representatives of the New Mexico U.S. Attorneys' Office have engaged in frequent outreach initiatives to tribal leaders and community members to inform them about the purpose and provisions of the Act. As part of their training and outreach, U.S. Attorney representatives encourage tribal leaders and citizens to report violations of the Act to Federal law enforcement for possible Federal prosecution. U.S. Attorneys' Office leadership has routinely discussed the Act and its consequences at District-wide Tribal Consultations and during the more than 50 training seminars and programs conducted throughout the District by the U.S. Attorneys' Office through the past two years.

The scope of the Indian Arts and Crafts Act changed dramatically over the years. The Act has been amended several times since its initial enactment in 1935. Amendments in 1990, 2000, and 2010 increased penalties, expanded enforcement from exclusive FBI jurisdiction to include all Federal law enforcement agencies and strengthened enforcement provisions. Application of the Act is not limited to retail sales of misrepresented goods. The Act can be used to address large-scale importations as we saw on the slides earlier. The 1990 Act also amended civil remedies and authorized civil suits by Indian tribes on behalf of themselves, individuals, as well as by Indian arts and crafts organizations. The 2010 amendments expanded civil enforcement by authorizing Indian arts and crafts organizations, as well as individual Indians, to file civil suits on their own. It also provided for civil lawsuits against manufacturers, wholesalers, and others involved in the distribution of the misrepresented product. Enabling Native Americans to pursue civil remedies independent from Federal law enforcement enhances the scope and deterrence of the Act.

United States Custom and Border Protection also has a role in maintaining the authenticity of Indian-style arts and crafts. Since 1990, CBP regulations require that imported Native American-style arts and crafts must generally be indelibly marked with a country of origin by cutting, die-sinking, engraving, stamping or some other comparable permanent identification. Investigations in these cases referred may require international assistance from foreign governments and the commitment of significant law enforcement re-sources.

Another means of protecting the integrity of Native-made arts and crafts is through trademarks used in commerce, which can be registered with the U.S. Patent and Trademark Office or a state by Indian artists, tribes, or arts and crafts organizations to identify authentic Indian products.

Finally, at least a dozen states, including New Mexico, have enacted laws prohibiting the sale of falsely labeled Indian arts and crafts. Under the state law of New Mexico, as you know very well, Vice Chairman, cases are being prosecuted both as misdemeanors and felonies, depending on the value of the item, or they may be the basis for permanent injunctive relief and court-ordered restitution.

Of course, one of the reasons for today's hearing is to discuss possible ways to modernize and improve the effectiveness of the Indian Arts and Crafts Act. The Department of Justice is always receptive to more effective legislative tools to help us protect the rights and public safety of Americans. We look forward to working with Congress to improve the Act.

Violations of the Indian Arts and Crafts Act currently cannot be prosecuted, for example, through the Federal money-laundering statutes, because these violations do not meet the definition of specified unlawful activities under the money-laundering statutes. The Federal money-laundering statutes are powerful tools to address the proceeds derived from criminal activity.

Finally, for felony prosecutions under the Act, the sale or price of the misrepresented goods or products must be, quote, "a total price of $1,000 or more." Because of the nature of the Indian arts and crafts business, many fraudulent dealers sell large quantities of misidentified products where each individual item sells for significantly less than $1,000, although gross sales of the misidentified items exceed the $1,000 threshold. Allowing for an aggregation of individual transactions would enable Federal prosecutors to more effectively prosecute large-scale distributors who violate the Act.

An example of this approach is Title 18, U.S. Section 641, the Theft of Public Money statute, which allows an aggregation of the value of property, money or things of value to reach the $1,000 threshold for felony prosecution.

On behalf of the Department of Justice, I wanted to thank the Committee for the opportunity to appear here today, and I'm happy to answer any questions. Thank you.

[The prepared statement of Ms. follows:]

PREPARED STATEMENT OF GRETCHEN C.F. SHAPPERT, ASSISTANT DIRECTOR, INDIAN, VIOLENT AND CYBER CRIME, EXECUTIVE OFFICE OF U.S. ATTORNEYS, U.S. DEPARTMENT OF JUSTICE

My name is Gretchen Shappert, and I am the Assistant Director of the Indian, Violent and Cyber Crime Staff in the Executive Office for U.S. Attorneys. On behalf of the Department of Justice and on behalf of my colleagues in the United States Attorney's Office (USAO) here in the District of New Mexico, I want to thank the Committee, Chairman Hoeven, and Vice-Chairman Udall for convening this important oversight field hearing. I also wish to thank the Santa Fe Indian School for hosting us today.

The Indian Arts and Crafts Act was enacted to protect Native American artists and artisans who rely on the creation and sale of traditional and contemporary art and craftwork to support their economic livelihood, preserve their unique heritage, and transfer their extraordinary culture and values to succeeding generations. Under the Act, it is illegal to sell art or craft products in a manner that falsely sug-gests that those products were produced by American Indians and Alaska Natives. A *2011 Government Accountably Office Report* concluded that the size of the In-dian arts and crafts markets and the extent of misrepresentation are unknown, in part because no national database specifically tracks Indian arts and crafts sales or misrepresentations. Furthermore, the GAO Report noted that U.S. federal and state laws protecting intellectual property do not explicitly include Native American and Alaska Native traditional knowledge and cultural expressions—such as processes for weaving baskets—and therefore provide little legal protection for them. Native American artisans have voiced concerns that the traditional knowledge of how to create Native arts and crafts—often passed down from generation to generation within the tribes—will not be carried forward by younger generations if they cannot make a living producing these goods. Hence, enforcement and education about the current Act is vital to ensuring the integrity of Native arts and crafts.

Here in the District of New Mexico, my colleagues in the USAO have used the criminal provisions of the Act, together with other federal criminal statutes, to pros-ecute misrepresentations of inauthentic items as genuine Indian arts and crafts. Two criminal prosecutions will demonstrate the significance of these cases. Andrew Gene Alvarez of Wofford Heights, California, was a prominent jeweler who alter-natively represented himself as Mescalero Apache, Colville, and Mayo Indian. He also used an alias, "Andrew 'Red Horse' Alvarez." He came to the attention of fed-eral law enforcement, because he was misrepresenting that the jewelry he was sell-ing at an art show in the Santa Fe Convention Center was made by an Indian. Mr. Alvarez was prosecuted under the Act, entered a guilty plea and was sentenced to 30 months of probation to be followed by a year of supervised release. As part of his sentence, he was prohibited from representing that any of the jewelry he pro-duced was of Indian origin. According to federal law enforcement officials in New Mexico, this prosecution was widely noted in the Native arts and crafts market, thereby serving as a potential deterrent to other potential fraudsters, who might be tempted to engage in similar conduct.

A second example of a criminal prosecution here in the District of New Mexico was the case of Rose Morris, who was sentenced to a probationary sentence of five years, following her guilty plea to two counts of misrepresentation of Indian pro-duced goods and products. Ms. Morris falsely claimed that the rugs she was selling were made by Native Americans, when in fact she randomly purchased the rugs from miscellaneous sources with no connection to Native craftsmen. In other cases, federal prosecutors have used a variety of federal statutes, such as wire fraud and mail fraud, to apprehend criminal offenders engaged in similar fraudulent conduct involving the misrepresentation of supposedly Indian arts and crafts.

Criminal prosecutions are not the only way that federal prosecutors support en-forcement of the Indian Arts and Crafts Act. Representatives of the New Mexico USAO have engaged in frequent outreach initiatives to tribal leaders and commu-nity members to inform them about the purpose and provisions of the Act. As part of their training and outreach, U.S. Attorney representatives encourage tribal lead-ers and citizens to report violations of the Act to federal law enforcement for pos-sible prosecution. USAO leadership has routinely discussed the Act and its con-sequences at District-wide Tribal Consultations and during the more than 50 train-ing seminars and programs conducted throughout the District by the USAO during the past two years.

The scope of the Indian Arts and Crafts Act has changed dramatically over the years. The Act has been amended several times since its initial enactment in 1935. Amendments in 1990, 2000, and 2010 increased penalties, *expanded enforcement from exclusive FBI jurisdiction to include any federal law enforcement agency, and strengthened enforcement provisions.* Application of the Act is not limited to retail sales of misrepresented goods. The Act can be used to address large-scale importa-tions by corporate distributors. The 1990 amendment also added civil remedies and authorized civil suits by an Indian tribe on behalf of itself, an individual Indian who is a member of the tribe, or an Indian arts and crafts organization. The 2010 *amendments* expanded civil enforcement by authorizing Indian arts and crafts orga-nizations, as well as individual Indians, to file civil suits on their own. It also pro-vided for civil law suits against manufacturers, wholesalers, and others involved in the distribution of the misrepresented product. Enabling Native Americans to pur-sue civil remedies independent from federal law enforcement enhances the scope and deterrence effects of the Act.

U.S. Customs and Border Protection (CBP) also has a role in maintaining the authenticity of Indian-style arts and crafts. Since 1990, *CBP regulations* require that imported Native American-style arts and crafts must generally be indelibly marked with the country of origin by cutting, die-sinking, engraving, stamping or some other comparable permanent identification. Investigations in these cases may require international assistance from foreign governments and the commitment of significant law enforcement resources.

Another means of protecting the integrity of Native-made arts and crafts is through trademarks used in commerce, which can be registered with the U.S. Patent and Trademark Office or a state by Indian artists, tribes, or arts and crafts organizations to identify authentic Indian products.

Finally, at least a dozen states—including New Mexico—have enacted laws prohibiting the sale of items falsely labelled as Indian arts and crafts. *Under the state law of New Mexico,* the sale or attempted sale of products falsely described as Indian labor or workmanship may be *prosecuted as a misdemeanor or felony,* depending upon the value of the items, or may be the basis for permanent injunctive relief and court-ordered restitution.

Of course, one of the reasons for today's hearing is to discuss possible ways to modernize and improve the effectiveness of the Indian Arts and Crafts Act. The Department of Justice is always receptive to more effective legislative tools to help us protect the rights and public safety of Americans. We look forward to working with Congress to improve the Act.

Second, violations of the Indian Arts and Crafts Act cannot currently be prosecuted through the federal money-laundering statutes, because these violations do not meet the statutory definition of specified unlawful activities under the money-laundering statutes. The federal money-laundering statutes are powerful tools to address the proceeds derived from criminal activity.

Finally, for felony prosecutions under the Act, the sale or price of the misrepresented good or product must be "a total price of $ 1,000 or more". Because of the nature of the Indian arts and crafts business, many fraudulent dealers sell large quantities of misidentified products where each individual items sells for significantly less than $ 1,000, although gross sales of the misidentified arts and crafts far exceed the $ 1,000 threshold. Allowing for an aggregation of individual transactions would enable federal prosecutors to more effectively prosecute large-scale distributors who violate the Act. An example of this approach is Title 18 USC ª 641, the Theft of Public Money statute, which allows for an aggregation of the value of property, money or things of value to reach the $ 1,000 threshold for felony prosecutions.

On behalf of the Department of Justice, I wanted to thank the Committee for the opportunity to appear before you this morning.

Senator UDALL. Thank you so much, Miss Shappert, and thank all the witnesses for traveling out and for being here and for your excellent testimony.

And we want to emphasize, from what you hear today, you can submit additions or addendums to your testimony as we move along. As several of you mentioned, as New Mexico's Attorney General, I prosecuted cases under state law that related to illegal sale of counterfeit Native American jewelry.

And at the time in the 1990s, it was estimated about 30 or 40 percent of the jewelry on the market was counterfeit. So it was a big problem then. But now I understand that as much as 80 percent of those goods are likely counterfeit and therefore being sold in violation of Federal law.

This doubling in a matter of decades is very alarming to me. So Chief Woody, can you provide an estimate on a percentage or even a range of the amount of counterfeit jewelry being sold in the local markets in New Mexico or in any other markets you're familiar with.

Mr. WOODY. I can tell you that Slide 1 showed you, that's all fraudulent. That is a hard—you know, it's very hard to get that figure. I don't know how you would go about doing it, because you have the legal market, you have the illegal market that gets mixed in, used as a cover, if you will, for all the illegal and really when we're working one of these enterprises at a time, it's focused on that, I don't know how you would extrapolate that out.

You know, I figure you throw out around 40, 50 percent back then, you know, I would speak to these cases. Yes, it's much higher. I can't tell you how much higher, because the retail market and retail stores are doing it. They could be as high as 80 percent, but that's a hard statement for me to make, sir.

Senator UDALL. And Miss Stanton, the primary purpose of the IACA is to protect Indian artists and businesses, tribal economics and culture. In fact, it was enacted in response to the growing influx of counterfeit Indian art and craftwork that was seriously eroding the market for authentic Indian products. How successful has the IACA been in fulfilling this purpose?

Ms. STANTON. Well, again, as I mentioned in the earlier testimony, we have had Federal prosecutions. So I think that is positive. And certainly, now working with the Fish and Wildlife Service, that number will dramatically rise. But a lot of what we do is try to educate the public and to try to send messages to the industry as well to prevent the sale.

That's really what we're focusing on in addition to law enforcement. So by better educating the consumer and sending messages to the overall industry, we think that we have made inroads with that. You saw on some of the slides that we have, we do consumer protection brochures. We instituted doing that in the New Mexico AG's office. We did that with the other state attorney general's offices. Also, we do a lot of work with the Federal Trade Commission, and we work with a lot of Indian organizations; whether it's the American Indian, Alaska Native Tourism Association, Indian Arts and Crafts Association.

So a lot of it is really focused on education and outreach. And, you know, we would love to do more. But we certainly feel that now that we're partnering with Fish and Wildlife Service, we're in a far better place.

Senator UDALL. Could you please elaborate a little bit, Miss Stanton, on the impacts of counterfeit Indian art on tribal communities, on their economy, on their social activity, and on their culture?

Ms. STANTON. Of course each community is different. Each tribe is different. But I think overall, especially in the Southwest, it's had really devastating effects economically, as I said, passing down the traditions. And certainly, Senator Campbell was very articulate in talking about how many people depend on this for a living; that it's so difficult to compete with the materials coming in from overseas. That is, it's what he says, depending on the dollar.

So it's frustrating. It's economically destabilizing, and a great deal needs to continue to be done and expanded on this effort.

Senator UDALL. Thank you for that.

Chief Woody, you've dedicated your career with the service to enforcement of Federal laws that protect endangered and threatened species, migratory birds, marine mammals, and global wildlife and plant resources. How did this service come to the investigative authority, have the investigative authority over the alleged violations of the IACA?

Mr. WOODY. Amendments to the Act. It allowed for any Federal law enforcement officer to investigate violations of the Act. And being a good friend of Miss Stanton's, her walking in the door with a cup of coffee helped an awful lot.

Senator UDALL. We appreciate that.

Under the MOIA how many law enforcement officers are currently assigned to investigate IACA violations? Is that enough to meet the overall demand?

Mr. WOODY. Officers that are working on it do the best they can with what they have. There is a dedicated—there are several dedicated officers who work on Indian arts and crafts issues. Also, we have—when we're doing the projects at certain points, we get help from HSI, FBI, every Federal agency that's tied into export-import into the country; State Department, strong support from DOJ, states, counties, county officials, local Native American tribes.

We get a lot of support on this work.

Senator UDALL. Could you talk a little bit more about the 2012 memorandum of agreement between the Fish and Wildlife Service and the IACB?

Mr. WOODY. Sure. Really what that is, the IABC essentially pays for the agents and the work they do. The agents work for Fish and Wildlife Service, they work for me, and we do the work. It's really, essentially—it's cost recovery for us, is what that MOA is.

Senator UDALL. Miss Stanton, it sounds like the MOA has helped address outstanding enforcement of the IACA somewhat, but are there more boots on the ground needed to adequately address the problem of trading on the Indian-made goods covered by the law?

Ms. STANTON. I would say that if additional agents were made available, they would have plenty to do.

Senator UDALL. And it looks like, Chief Woody, you agree with that.

Mr. WOODY. Yes, I do.

Senator UDALL. Miss Shappert, do you also?

Ms. SHAPPERT. I will defer to my law enforcement colleagues as to the resources they needed.

Senator UDALL. Great. Thank you very much. Thank you for your testimony.

Senator Heinrich, the floor is yours for questions.

Senator HEINRICH. Thank you, Vice Chairman Udall.

Chief, when you find a case like this when large amounts of jewelry are coming into the country fraudulently labeled, are you able to seize those shipments under the current statute?

Mr. WOODY. They are seized for evidence, yes.

Senator UDALL. Can you seize them on forfeiture?

Mr. WOODY. On forfeiture, no.

Senator HEINRICH. Would it be helpful to have an amendment to the statute that addressed that particularly?

Mr. WOODY. We would be more than happy to sit down with you and look at that very closely. You know, one thing we don't want—when you're dealing with—look at it this way. You don't want a criminal enterprise to look at penalties in the Act, just consider it a cost of doing business.

Senator HEINRICH. Absolutely.

Mr. WOODY. In other words, you know, they look at the fine, and they say—you know, we're talking $11 million in this particular case. $250,000 is really a pittance on them. You know, is that a cost of doing business for the criminal enterprise? Yeah, I'd say. You want to look at enhancements to the Act, and you want that Act to act as a deterrent, if you will, just knowing what's in it.

Senator HEINRICH. Miss Shappert mentioned potential changes to the Federal money-laundering definition to allow to meet the definition. The aggregation of value to meet the thousand-dollar threshold. Are there similar changes that you can think of, Chief, that would, that you bumped up against in the—in trying to prosecute these cases or investigate these cases?

Mr. WOODY. As Gretchen stated, that is one of the ones we've talked about a bit amongst the officers, the agents, and us. But having policy discussions, we need—again, I'm more than happy— or someone is more than happy to sit down with you on technical issues.

Senator HEINRICH. You concur that those two changes would be helpful?

Mr. WOODY. Yes.

Senator HEINRICH. Great.

In the Al Zuni case, did we have cooperation from Philippine law enforcement?

Mr. WOODY. Yes, we did. We had good cooperation from the Philippine government.

Senator HEINRICH. Is that possible, apart, because of Fish and Wildlife's role in also working with foreign countries, in Southeast Asia and other places in wildlife trafficking issues?

Mr. WOODY. Yeah. In the last several years, we've been able to put agents out throughout the world. We have fellow agents that are attachés stationed in a number of countries; the Asian countries, Africa, working on a number of issues. They're working strongly—a lot of work we do in the Philippines, we've built long-term, good relationships there.

And yes, that helped immensely.

Senator HEINRICH. Miss Stanton, you went through some of the educational efforts that you are currently pursuing to give people the knowledge to know the difference. Are you pursuing a similar strategy online as what you've done with print, kiosks, and other places in the state of New Mexico?

Ms. STANTON. Well, in particular, we worked closely with the legal departments of a number of online marketing platforms. That would be Amazon, Etsy, eBay, and Artfire, in particular. And we had a lot of complaints about online marketing, I will tell you that, and we really value the complaints we get from the public, and we try to do our own monitoring as well. But it is extensive, the problems with Internet marketing.

What we typically do is, once we see potential violations, we will reach out to the vendor, and that's the first real collaboration with that platform, and they will provide the contact information, and then we will do our due diligence in trying to determine the extent of the violation and communicating with that vendor on how to comply.

If they don't comply, we have them dropped. So that's one of the really good vehicles that we have to monitor online marketing.

Senator HEINRICH. How often—what has the relationship been like with some of those large online vendor platforms?

Ms. STANTON. EBay in particular was really our first agreement. And they've been excellent. And there are some challenges every step of the way, but Etsy now has come around, and we've been working with them, and Amazon, who's massive, and Artfire. So whenever we have the opportunity, we reach out and try to get collaborations with their legal departments.

Senator HEINRICH. For any of you, really, do you have a sense for how oftentimes a retail store or a vendor knows that what they're marketing is actually fraudulently labeled?

Ms. STANTON. Well, I certainly think in the operation of the Al Zuni case, everybody was understanding what was going on. It's— you know, greed does a lot of things to people.

Senator HEINRICH. Miss Shappert, I wanted to ask you, the 2011 GAO report cites that there isn't a national database to track these kinds of Indian arts and crafts sales. Is that true, and should there be a database to track this kind of thing?

Ms. SHAPPERT. To be honest, Senator, I think it points to a problem. I don't know if there could be a database, because of the individuality of the art. So I think it underscores the challenges associated with these kind of investigations, and that's one of the reasons, because the art is so individualized between different tribes.

Senator HEINRICH. Okay. I want to thank you all for your testimony.

Senator UDALL. Thank you very much, Senator Heinrich.

Miss Stanton, the expansion of retail sales online has changed the face of commerce and allowed consumers incredible access to products around the world and around the globe. But I imagine this access presents the challenges with respect to online sales of Native arts and crafts and IACA enforcement.

Does the Board's mission to promote Indian economic development through expansion of Native art and craft market include e-commerce? A simple Google search reveals online retailers, such as Etsy and eBay, selling goods as vintage or authentic Native American jewelry. Does the IACA provide the tools necessary to enforce violations with e-commerce?

Ms. STANTON. Well, a violation is a violation. And so whether it's occurring on eBay or Etsy or Downtown Santa Fe or—you know, we treat it all equally. And as I mentioned, we work with the legal departments of these online platforms. And we feel well served. But there's still so much to do. It just really is a tremendous problem.

Senator UDALL. Does the IACB certify reputable online retailers?

Ms. STANTON. We have a source directory of American Indian and Alaska Native-owned and operated arts and crafts businesses. To be listed in that directory, you have to be a member of a federally recognized tribe and provide your tribal documentation. And that's a free opportunity for Indian artists to promote their work, and we publish that online.

Senator UDALL. Do you think the IACB should certify reputable online retailers?

Ms. STANTON. We could certainly look into that. We have not done so thus far, but we'd be happy to do that.

Senator UDALL. Do you believe that these fraudulent online sales, are they a significant problem?

Ms. STANTON. Yes.

Senator UDALL. Yes. What is the extent of that problem, as far as your knowledge of it?

Ms. STANTON. I couldn't give you a percentage. But I can tell you from the complaints we receive every day, that authentic Indian artists and authentic Indian art businesses are not happy at all, because of the competition.

Senator UDALL. For the record, would you be able to give us some numbers on the numbers of complaints that you have gotten?

Ms. STANTON. Oh, absolutely.

Senator UDALL. That would be very helpful.

Chief, do you have any comment in this area?

Mr. WOODY. We do a lot of work on the Internet, whether wildlife work or some of this other. As Meredith stated, it is immense. I think there are some pretty good tools out there that you may be aware of. We're working online, and we've got some backup. Customs and Border Patrol and DHS has been absolutely a good partner working with us on these cases.

They have a location called Commercial Targeting Analysis Center. We'll have agents work online, and you can move it over to the Commercial Targeting Analysis Center. And you can focus on some really specific things off of that. There's a lot of good things going on behind the scenes.

I welcome you out, when you're back in D.C. at any time, we'd be more than happy to show you some of those locations and the great work that goes on behind the scenes there.

Senator UDALL. We should probably have a visit and take a look at that. That would be very helpful.

Mr. WOODY. I look forward to it, sir.

Senator UDALL. Do tribal governments play a role or could they play a role in certifying authentic Native American arts and crafts for sale online?

Ms. STANTON. They certainly could. They sometimes do have their own version of a certification program. I know the Cherokee in Oklahoma, and in a different forum that we talked about in Oklahoma, have similar issues as well as—I think that perhaps the Cherokee in North Carolina.

Senator UDALL. Chief, have—and also to Miss Shappert—have any charges been brought against retailers for violating the IACA for online sales or any pending?

Mr. WOODY. Not that I am aware of, off the top of my head.

Ms. SHAPPERT. Not that I'm aware of.

Mr. WOODY. Not that we're working on.

Senator UDALL. Do you have agents that are looking for illegal activity online?

Mr. WOODY. Depends on what the agents are working on. Assigned to the cases they're working on right now, yes. But talking specifically, that—I can't answer that question.

Senator UDALL. Do you think it would be helpful to dedicate resources to improving fraudulent—to looking at the fraudulent online sales?

Mr. WOODY. With the right information coming in, absolutely, yes.

Senator UDALL. Miss Shappert?

Ms. SHAPPERT. We would be delighted, in the Department of Justice, to review anything that our colleagues in Fish and Wildlife bring to us from their online searches for possible Federal prosecution.

Senator UDALL. Okay, great.

I'd like to turn to the recent Fish and Wildlife Service investigation known as Operation Al Zuni that's been reported as the largest investigation ever into fraudulent Native American jewelry sales under the Indian Arts and Crafts Act.

As reported in the press, this case involves individuals who established and operated manufacturing facilities in the Philippines in order to market and sell Native American-style jewelry and handicrafts as authentic Indian-made. Counterfeit Indian-made jewelry, in particular, was sold in stores located in Albuquerque and Santa Fe with heavy tourist foot traffic.

So from Miss Shappert and Chief Woody, I know this is an ongoing investigation, but to the extent you can answer, does Operation Al Zuni—does that investigation go deeper than the individuals who were indicted earlier this year?

In other words, are more indictments coming in this case?

Ms. SHAPPERT. With all due respect, we cannot comment on ongoing investigations.

Senator UDALL. Chief, you're in the same position on that one?

Mr. WOODY. Yes, sir.

Senator UDALL. And I would just advise everybody to look at the reporting that's out there, because there's some very good reporting that I think elucidates some of these issues, and we'll look forward to be following what's going on.

Is DOJ and Fish and Wildlife Service prioritizing this investigation, and would you characterize this case to be part of a broader network of counterfeiters?

Mr. WOODY. The case is prioritized. We have had—New Mexico Attorneys' Office has been absolutely top-notch with this. It is a priority. There are a number of cases out there being worked.

Senator UDALL. Okay. Good. I wanted to have that for the record.

You testified that the declared value of sales in fraudulent Native American-style jewelry related to this investigation is 11 million. But is that the retail value or is it substantially higher?

Mr. WOODY. That's the declared value coming into the U.S. I would say maybe Meredith can answer this better. You know, whether it's a wholesale after that or retail after that, it's substantially much higher. So that is the declared value when it comes into the U.S.

Senator UDALL. Is there a way to—please go ahead.

Ms. STANTON. I don't think it would be farfetched to say that the 11 million easily turns into double that.

Senator UDALL. So that's your best guess at this point.

Ms. STANTON. Yes, sir.

Senator UDALL. Chief, would you argue with that?

Mr. WOODY. No, I would not argue with Meredith.

Senator UDALL. And obviously, this is an enormous amount of money that should be going back to Indian Country. Native jewelers and artisans rely on their works to earn a living, provide for their families and sustain their cultural expression and identities from generation to generation, not to mention its impact on consumer confidence in the Indian art market.

In other words, this is not a victimless crime. Miss Shappert and Chief Woody, what are your agencies doing to combat the spread of violations of the IACA?

Ms. SHAPPERT. Well, I reference to you—first of all, Chief Woody has talked about some of the things that his agency is doing in collaboration with the Department of Justice. And I know from my colleagues in the U.S. Attorneys' Office in New Mexico, they are extremely grateful for their close partnership with Fish and Wildlife, which goes into many different areas of prosecution.

We talked about the importance of deterrence, and part of that is, Meredith referred to us getting the message out. The U.S. Attorneys' Office in New Mexico and other U.S. Attorneys' Offices are engaged in that. They make a point of emphasizing the Indian Arts and Crafts Act in their trainings, their tribal consultations, and their meetings with other law enforcement partners so that we could discourage this type of activity.

And as we saw in the Alvarez prosecution, when these cases are prosecuted, it does send a chill through the minds of those who might be tempted to commit these kind of crimes.

Senator UDALL. Anything to add?

Ms. STANTON. I totally agree. The deterrent value of these investigations and prosecutions, they're just—it's priceless.

Senator UDALL. In your testimony, you state that, "The scope of the counterfeiting problem is far larger than expected."

Are there other IACA investigations ongoing, and could you please describe them, and are they limited to the United States, or is there an international component? Or is that one that we shouldn't be getting into?

Mr. WOODY. There are other cases, and there's an international.

Senator UDALL. Good, good.

Well, we really appreciate your effort on this front and look forward to sharing and visiting with you, as you talked about, in terms of making this a top priority and also making sure that the people targeted are the ones that are doing the most damage.

Senator Heinrich?

Senator HEINRICH. Miss Shappert, I wanted to ask you, you mentioned a couple of cases, including the case of Mr. Alvarez, that resulted in probation being handed out. Do you think that the punishments typically imposed under the Indian Arts and Crafts Act typically provide an adequate deterrent?

Ms. SHAPPERT. Well, I can tell you the punishments provided are what the Act currently provides. And with the current sentencing guideline configuration, the inclination would probably be, in most cases, if someone doesn't have a record, I'm speculating that they would not get active prison time. But that's another reason why the financial component of the punishment must be significant.

Because, as important as prison is for many kinds of crimes, hitting people in the pocketbook is a real chilling deterrent for many fraudsters.

Senator HEINRICH. And do you find that that portion of the penalties handed out typically does have that kind of impact?

Ms. SHAPPERT. Well, as I indicated in my testimony, we're very interested in the possibility of having conversations with the Committee, including on things like aggregation of the penalties so that you could go after individuals more effectively who were engaged in large-scale amounts of money.

And Chief Woody referred to forfeiture as something to be considered. Asset forfeiture is a powerful tool for dealing with fraud and other types of crime when you can go after the instrumentalities and the profits and the large monetary base of these operations.

We are happy to have any conversations with the Committee that they would like to have about these issues.

Senator HEINRICH. I suspect the Committee looks forward to that.

Chief, does your collaboration extend to BIA law enforcement, given their tribal relationships?

Mr. WOODY. To date, we have not worked—we've worked with them on some of the operations when they're coming to conclusion, working—the investigators working. We do not have anybody working with us at BIA at this point.

That's not to say—we're open for those conversations with BIA in the future.

Senator HEINRICH. It sounds like a lot of this is really coordination working across multiple agencies; U.S. Attorneys, Attorneys General, Fish and Wildlife Service, you mentioned Customs and Border Protection.

Mr. WOODY. It is excellent cooperation.

Senator HEINRICH. That's great.

Much of the conversation today has focused on jewelry. To what extent does this same sort of enforcement extend to things like textiles, pottery, ceramics, and other tribal Native American arts and crafts?

Ms. STANTON. Well, certainly we have complaints about all media; very contemporary work; very traditional works, weavings, masks, carvings. In fact, these are from one of the five indictments in Alaska. And so it's all across the board.

Senator HEINRICH. Can you tell us a little bit about what those are?

Mr. WOODY. Yes. So in this particular case—and again, to get to the crux of these cases—you're putting people undercover and working these. I'm looking at the back of these, and on this particular one on my right, to your left, you've got a price tag of $1,700. And then you've another tag that says, "Authentic Native handicraft from Alaska," and a third sticker that says, "Made in Alaska."

Just looking at that, you're not going to know it. But again, working behind the scenes and getting to the fraud that went into making this, putting those stickers on, that's what we focus our investigations on doing. There were a number of items similar to this that were seized in the case, and actually, the complaint came in from some tourists on what was going on behind the scenes, and that we worked on this case.

Senator HEINRICH. Well, I want to thank you all again for your testimony today. I'm going to have to leave right now, but I'm going to leave you in the Vice Chairman's very capable hands.

Senator UDALL. Thank you, Senator Heinrich. I really appreciate you spending so much time with us here this morning.

And let me once again just thank the witnesses. And you're certainly invited to stay and listen to the second panel. I know you may be busy and heading off to other things, but really, really appreciate your travels and testimony here today.

We're going to take just a five-minute break to rearrange name tags and to sort out things up here. And so we excuse this panel, and we have a short recess and call up the next panel, which is Damon Martinez, Joyce Begay-Foss, Mr. Dallin, and Harvey Pratt. Thank you very much.

[Recess from 11:41 a.m. to 11:59 a.m.]

Senator UDALL. Okay. Let's have everybody sit down. Any conversations that are going on, we hope that you will move those off the floor a little bit. We understand people had a little bit hard time, especially the court reporter. So we really urge you to stay very close to your microphone. And I may remind you a little bit every now and then or the people behind me may say, "Speak up," or "Move in" like that to the microphone.

I just very briefly, before I introduce our second panel and proceed with them, I would like to recognize—there have been many tribal officials that have visited here today, in and out. And I want to recognize the very, very good leadership they have given on this issue in Indian Country.

And we have a number of them that have been here this morning. Governor Mark Mitchell, with Tesuque; Governor Peter Garcia, Ohkay Owingeh; First Lieutenant Governor Mac Zuni with Isleta; Second Lieutenant Governor Marvin Trujillo, Laguna; Councilman Gil Vigil, with Tesuque; Ben Chavarria, Tribal Historic Preservation office, Santa Clara; Second Lieutenant Governor Matt Martinez, Ohkay Owingeh.

We've got Councilman Pascal Anjade, Mescalero Apache; Lieutenant Governor Jerome Lucero, Zia Pueblo. And also from the Navajo Nation, Barbara Mago. She's the Native arts and crafts director there.

Let me just say once again to our second panel, thank you for coming, and thank you for traveling here. We really appreciate having you here today. We have Mr. Damon Martinez, the former U.S. Attorney for the District of New Mexico; Miss Joyce Begay-Foss, director, Living Traditions Education Center at the Museum of Indian Arts & Culture right here located in Santa Fe; Mr. Dallin Maybee, chief operating officer Southwest Association for Indian Arts; and Mr. Harvey Pratt, a Native American artist and retired forensic artist from Oklahoma.

Thank you for coming. I look forward to hearing your testimony, beginning with Mr. Martinez.

Please proceed.

STATEMENT OF DAMON MARTINEZ, FORMER U.S. ATTORNEY, DISTRICT OF NEW MEXICO, U.S. DEPARTMENT OF JUSTICE

Mr. MARTINEZ. Good afternoon, Chairman Udall. It is a great honor to testify before this Committee regarding the Indian Arts and Crafts Act. I also want to thank the Santa Fe School for hosting this field hearing.

In New Mexico, we are very privileged to have Native American art and craftwork that reflects generations of unique culture and a rich heritage. In the 1990s, as an assistant Attorney General for the State of New Mexico, I gained an appreciation for the difference that government can make when I watched you as Attorney General protect Native American artists and artisans from dishonest practices.

Now, after having served as a U.S. Attorney for New Mexico, I submit it is important for law enforcement—including the U.S. Attorneys' Office—to prioritize its limited resources on prosecuting those who knowingly counterfeit Native American art and craftwork.

To accomplish this effectively, Federal law needs to provide the necessary tools to investigate and prosecute those who exploit and undermine the cultural heritage of Native Americans. In modernizing the Indian Arts and Crafts Act, I have proposed—I have respectfully proposed to this Committee seven recommendations for your consideration.

Mr. Vice Chairman, also at this point, I would like to take the opportunity, having served in the U.S. Attorneys' Office, there's two people that I want to recognize from the U.S. Attorneys' Office. These are the ones who are incredible public servants, and the job that they do on behalf of the community, on behalf of the nation, they never receive credit for it. Those two people right now are Christopher Houghton and Jonathan Gersen who are in the audience today. They are true public servants, and they deserve credit for the work that they do.

And at this point, I would just answer any questions you have on the second set of recommendations that I'll make, or any other questions that you would wish to propose.

[The prepared statement of Mr. Martinez follows:]

PREPARED STATEMENT OF DAMON MARTINEZ, FORMER U.S. ATTORNEY, DISTRICT OF NEW MEXICO, U.S. DEPARTMENT OF JUSTICE

Good morning. Chairman Hoeven, Vice Chairman Udall, Senator Heinrich, and members of the Committee on Indian Affairs, it is a great honor to testify before the Committee regarding the Indian Arts and Crafts Act.

In New Mexico, we are very privileged to have Native American art and craftwork that reflects generations of unique culture and a rich heritage. In the 1990s, as an Assistant Attorney General for the State of New Mexico, I gained an appreciation for the difference that government can make when I watched then Attorney General Tom Udall protect Native American artists and artisans from dishonest practices. Now, after having served as the U.S. Attorney for New Mexico, I submit it is im- portant for law enforcement, including the U.S. Attorney's Office, to prioritize its' limited resources on prosecuting those who knowingly counterfeit Native American art and craftwork. To accomplish this effectively, federal law needs to provide the necessary tools to investigate and prosecute those who exploit and undermine the cultural heritage of Native Americans.

In modernizing the Indian Arts and Crafts Act (the "Act"), I respectfully propose the following recommendations for your consideration to make the law a more comprehensive and effective tool.

First, the Act should consider the importation of Native American-style merchandise into the commerce of the United States separate from the sale of Native American-style merchandise in the United States.

Second, the Act should require clearly and simply that Native American-style merchandise imported into the commerce of the United States must have an indelible country-of-origin marking. Currently, a prosecutor must look to 19 C.F.R. 134.43(c)("Method and Location of Marking Imported Articles"), and 18 U.S.C. §§ 542 ("Entry of goods by means of false statements") and 545 ("Smuggling goods into the United States") to establish this requirement.

Third, the Act should require that the seller of Native American-style merchandise in the United States have a basis for representing that such merchandise is actually Native American produced.

Fourth, the Act should have a specific forfeiture section. Currently, a prosecutor must look to 18 U.S.C. §§ 1341 (Fraud and Swindles), and 1342 (Fraud by wire, radio, or television) to seek forfeiture.

Fifth, 18 U.S.C. § 1956 (Laundering of monetary instruments) should be amended to include a violation of 18 U.S.C. § 1159 (Misrepresentation of Indian produced goods and products) as a specified unlawful activity.

Sixth, 18 U.S.C. § 2516(1)(c) (Authorization for interception of wire, oral, or electronic communications) should be amended to include 18 U.S.C. § 1159 (Misrepresentation of Indian produced goods and products) as an offense for investigation.

And finally, the U.S. Department of Homeland Security should be encouraged to flag or seize during custom inspections Native American-style merchandise imported into the commerce of the United States that does not have an indelible country-of-origin marking on each item of merchandise.

Thank you for your consideration of my recommendations and I stand ready to answer any questions the Committee members may have.

Senator UDALL. Thank you. Thank you very much.

And Mr. Pratt, please proceed.

And we'll get to questions after we go through the entire panel and their testimony.

STATEMENT OF HARVEY PRATT, CHEYENNE-ARAPAHO MASTER ARTIST

Mr. PRATT. Good afternoon, Vice Chairman Udall. My name is Harvey Pratt, and I'm pleased to testify before you today. I'm a Cheyenne-Arapaho master artist from Oklahoma, on the Board of the Red Earth Festival, which represents a large annual Indian art market in Oklahoma City. I recently retired with over 50 years in law enforcement from the Oklahoma State Bureau of Investigation. While I was also—while I am also the Indian Arts and Crafts Board chairman, I am testifying today solely on my capacity as a private citizen and as a Cheyenne chief. My recommendations are my own and do not in any way reflect the official position of the Board or the Department of the Interior.

Indian art is not just a commodity. Indian art reflects who we are, where we came from, where we're going. It's a reflection of our beliefs, religion, legends, and lifestyle. You can see these connections in the kachina carvings, paintings of Green Corn Dances, Native American Church fans and rattles, and Spider Woman's role in weavings, to name a few.

Art is also about healing. For example, following an alarming number of Indian youths committing suicide in record number, all that, at the invitation of the Board's Southern Plains Indian Museum, I provided a workshop at the museum to encourage the Indian youth and their families to constructively cope with these tragedies.

Indian art is also about being able to provide important income for our families to carry on traditions of our ancestors in contemporary and a challenging world. I know from firsthand experience about the importance of promoting and protecting Indian artists and their creativity and about the importance of Indian Arts and Crafts Act enforcement.

When Indian artists are undercut by the sale of fake Indian art, the integrity of authentic Indian art and artists suffer. We're also being robbed economically, culturally, and spiritually. These unscrupulous businesses are also ripping off consumers and the viability of the Indian art. An example would be my brother Charles Pratt, an internationally known Cheyenne-Arapaho sculptor, residing in New Mexico, made a bronze chess set featuring cowboys and Indians. It was later purchased and knocked off by a non-Indian, who then duplicated it and sold it as Indian art.

Though many Indian artists do not have the resources to fight these injustices, fortunately, Charles did and was compensated by his loss by taking this individual to court. And after the hearing of this, I too support the modernization of the Act to better protect the artists and the Indian art industry. When Charles was confronted by this man, he told him that he had been doing this over 30 years and had never been confronted before.

Although the State of Oklahoma does not provide State tribal recognition status, state recognized tribes have been a significant issue in Oklahoma. This is due to the fact that, unlike the Federal tribal recognition procedures, there is no such standard for official state tribal recognition. State tribal recognition requirements dramatically vary among those states that provide such recognition.

Inconsistency in recognizing criteria also affects New Mexico Indian artists as well as Indian artists nationwide. Artists from federally recognized tribes are often selling their art next to artists from tribes that may or may not be officially recognized by a state. These artists may also consider their tribe officially recognized by a state, even if the state does not. A clear, easily verifiable standard within the statute would benefit all Indian artists.

As an Indian artist, I also firmly support any effort to expand the Act investigative program conducted by the Board through their agreement with the U.S. Fish and Wildlife Service on behalf of Indian artists, businesses, and tribes, as well as consumers.

In addition, I support education and educating all appropriate Federal law enforcement about the Act and the need to protect Indian artists and collectors from fraudulent activity. When state tourism and the economy are so dependent on Indian artists and culture, here where such a high percentage of Indian artists are distributed to businesses and consumers nationwide, I believe that strengthening the Act would not only benefit your constituents but consumers nationwide.

Senator UDALL. thank you for the opportunity to share my thoughts with you.

[The prepared statement of Mr. Pratt follows:]

PREPARED STATEMENT OF HARVEY PRATT, CHEYENNE-ARAPAHO MASTER ARTIST

Good Morning Vice Chairman Udall and Senator Heinrich. My name is Harvey Pratt and I am pleased to testify before you today.

I am a Cheyenne-Arapaho master artist, a traditional Peace Chief of the Southern Cheyenne Chief's Lodge, and on the Board of the Red Earth Inc., which runs a large annual Indian art market in Oklahoma City. I recently retired following over 50 years in law enforcement with the Oklahoma State Bureau of Investigation.

I come from a long line of Indian artists. My brother is internationally known Cheyenne-Arapaho sculptor and New Mexico resident, Charlie Pratt, and my mother, Cheyenne storyteller and educator Ann Pratt Shadlow, received the honor of Native American Woman of the Year in 1987.

While I am also the Indian Arts and Crafts Board Chairman, I am testifying today solely in my capacity as a private citizen, and my comments are my own and do not in any way reflect the official position of the Board or the Department of the Interior.

Indian art is not just a commodity. Indian art reflects who we are, where we came from, and where we are going. It reflects our beliefs, religions, legends, and life ways. You can see these connections in our kachina carvings, paintings of Green Corn Dances, Native American Church fans and rattles, and in Spider Woman's role in weavings, to name a few.

Indian art is also about healing. For example, I had the great pleasure of participating in a three-day event sponsored by the Board's Southern Plains Indian Museum in Anadarko, Oklahoma. This event, supported by the surrounding Indian tribes, was held to help address an alarming number of Indian youth suicides affecting every member of the community. I spoke to the children and their families about the importance of the arts in the healing process, and provided a painting workshop to engage the children and encourage them to constructively cope with the tragedies of losing family members and friends.

Indian art is also about being able to provide important income for our families and to carry on traditions of our ancestors in a contemporary and challenging world. I know from first-hand experience about the importance of promoting and pro- tecting Indian artists and their creative work, and about the importance of Indian Arts and Crafts Act enforcement.

When Indian artists are undercut by the sale of fake Indian art, the integrity of authentic Indian art and artists suffer. We are being robbed economically, culturally, and spiritually. These unscrupulous businesses are also ripping off consumers and the viability of the Indian market.

Time and time again, I hear from my fellow Indian artists about their art and craftwork being knocked off by nonIndians and sold as Indian made. In fact, my brother Charles Pratt made and sold a bronze chess set featuring cowboy and Indian chess pieces. Later, Charles discovered that the purchaser had reproduced that chess set in silver without his approval, and was selling the reproductions to galleries as Charles' work. Many Indian artists do not have the resources to pursue these cases. Fortunately, Charles was able to take the man to court, stop the reproduction, and was compensated for the sales. The purchaser later told Charles that he had been knocking off others work for over 30 years, and no one had previously challenged him.

As the title of this hearing conveys, I too believe that "modernizing", in other words strengthening, the Act would greatly benefit Indian artists and the Indian art industry.

I support removing any obstacles or unintended loopholes that have hindered Act investigations and enforcement. For example, as an Indian artist I believe the statute's current definition of State recognized tribe should be reexamined and revised.

Although the State of Oklahoma does not provide State tribal recognition status, State recognized tribes have been a significant issue in Oklahoma. This is due to the fact that, unlike the federal tribal recognition process, there is no such standard for official State tribal recognition, and State tribal recognition requirements dramatically vary among those states that provide such recognition.

Inconsistency in recognition criteria also affects New Mexico Indian artists, as well as Indian artists nationwide. Artists from federally recognized tribes often are selling their art next to artists from tribes that may, or may not, be officially recognized by a State. Those artists may also consider their tribe officially recognized by a State, even if the State does not. A clear, easily verifiable standard within the statute would benefit all Indian artists.

As an Indian artist, I also firmly support any efforts to expand the Act investigative program conducted by the Board through their agreement with the U.S. Fish and Wildlife Service's Office of Law Enforcement on behalf of Indian artists, businesses, and tribes, as well as consumers.

In addition, I support educating all appropriate federal law enforcement about the Act and the need to protect Indian artists and the collectors from fraudulent activity.

Here in New Mexico, where the State's tourism and economy are so dependent on Indian art, artists, and culture, and here where such a high percentage of Indian

art is distributed to businesses and consumers nationwide, I believe that strengthening the Act would not only benefit your constituents, but consumers nationwide.
Senators Udall and Heinrich, thank you for the opportunity to share my thoughts
and concerns with you today.

Senator UDALL. Thank you so much, Mr. Pratt.
And let's proceed. Mr. Maybee, please.

STATEMENT OF DALLIN MAYBEE, CHIEF OPERATING OFFICER, SOUTHWESTERN ASSOCIATION FOR INDIAN ARTS (SWAIA)

Mr. MAYBEE. Thank you, Vice Chair. I appreciate the opportunity to come and speak a little bit about my experiences and insights and perceptions of the Indian Arts and Crafts Act and its
implications on the contemporary Native American art world.

My name is Dallin Maybee. I am Northern Arapaho and Seneca.
I grew up on the Cattaraugus reservation in Western New York,
but I'm actually enrolled in the Wind River Agency up in central
Wyoming. I am the chief operating officer for the Southwestern Association for Indian Arts, the nonprofit that produces the 96 year-
old Santa Fe Indian Market. I have a background in Native American performing arts and visual arts and, of course, in Federal Indian law.

The Indian Arts and Crafts Act was a welcome addition to the
world of Indian art. It was meant to be a buffer and a safeguard
to the economic opportunities of our communities. Artists have
been able to see firsthand the significance of the Act as they
produce art forms and narratives that often present aspects of their
cultural identity that they choose to share with the world.

As a participating artist at the Santa Fe Indian Market, my eyes
were opened to the economic opportunity that the Native art market offered, as people appreciated my creativity and continuation of
art forms that we have often been practicing for generations. Often
utilitarian in usage, some everyday art forms have evolved into fine
art forms in which our artists are able to receive suitable compensation for. But like most perceived opportunities were gained,
many of these forms have been copied and reproduced, robbed of
the Native soul and creativity that often accompanies authenticity.

The nonprofit that produces the Santa Fe Indian Market, we hold
a venerated and prestigious place amongst all the now-inter-
ested in Native American fine art markets. We are the oldest and
had humble beginnings in 1922. And for almost 96 years, artists
from predominately the Southwest and now tribes from throughout
North America and Canada descend upon the Santa Fe community,
the traditional homelands of Tesuque, and other pueblos here in
New Mexico, to not only enjoy the beautiful scenery and the fine
food, but also to experience Native America at its finest.

And it's presented through the many fine art forms we see. We
also, as part of our programming, produce everything from couture
and traditional fashion to food to performing arts. We cooperate
with and partner with the National Museum of the American Indian to present a film festival. All of these things cooperates to create an experience unlike any other, with an economic impact of almost $80 million upon the state of New Mexico itself and the city
of Santa Fe.

When we engage with our visitors, they indicate that they come to Santa Fe simply to experience what Native America has to offer. As thought leaders for a constantly evolving dynamic of how peo‐ple define Native art, our foundation is the artists themselves. We currently accept artists from across the United States and Canada, and we do require that participating artists provide proof of enroll‐ment or, as per the Act, evidence of tribal certification from the tribe that they claim descendancy. This definition of how we define who is Indian, as Senator Campbell indicated, is still a challenge almost 30 years later. We routinely hear of artists who have legiti‐mate descendancy, either from their mother or their father's side.

But my own example, for instance, if I was not enrolled on my mother's side—even though I was half Seneca—my father is a full‐blooded Seneca—it's a matriarchal enrollment process. I would not find a place at Santa Fe Indian Market or elsewhere to be able to say, "As a Native American, I am producing art, and you can, therefore, buy it."

I would be precluded from the Act.

Some of the challenges that we see at Indian Market for our art‐ists is the appropriation that occurs, not only from the theft of de‐sign, but also from the wholesale theft of often cultural identity. On occasion we find artists who submit for consideration their applica‐tion claiming descendancy in order to come to Indian Market and take advantage of the economic benefit that our market has, but they simply on any level are not Native, either through descendancy or enrollment.

So the first challenge that we see would be in the definitions of the Indian Arts and Crafts Act. How do you define who is an In‐dian? And we create models and mechanisms for tribes often to participate or adapt or evolve in order to help them create a certifi‐cation process for themselves. We want to exercise our sovereignty, but oftentimes we lack the resources or the knowledge to create the models ourselves.

So if we see successful models from Cherokee or the Choctaw in Oklahoma, we would hope that we'd be able to create forms or en‐gage with them in order to create models for other tribes that need assistance on that form.

The testimony today is also reflected heavily on enforcement. While we have seen a lot of success on both sides of that issue of either dealers engaging in fraudulent representation of Indian art or artists themselves engaging in fraudulent identity, there just simply needs to be more enforcement. I won't spend too much time on that because I think it's been stressed quite a bit.

But again, I am grateful for the opportunity to present my expe‐riences with the Indian Arts and Crafts Act. The challenges are definitely many, but through further definition and clarification, I think we can continue to step forward and protect the interests of our Native artists and their art forms. Thank you.

[The prepared statement of Mr. Maybee follows:]

PREPARED STATEMENT OF DALLIN MAYBEE, CHIEF OPERATING OFFICER, SOUTHWESTERN ASSOCIATION FOR INDIAN ARTS (SWAIA)

Good morning, my name is Dallin Maybee, I am Northern Arapaho and Seneca from the Spoonhunter and Maybee family's. I am the Chief Operating Officer of the

Southwestern Association for Indian Arts (SWAIA), the non-profit that produces the world-renowned Santa Fe Indian Market, which is currently in its 96th year. I have an extensive background in Native American performing arts, in the visual arts, and in Federal Indian law.

I would like to thank the Senate Committee on Indian Affairs for the opportunity to speak to you today about my experience and insights on the Indian Arts and Crafts Act.

The Indian Arts and Crafts Act was a welcome addition to the world of Indian Art. Meant to be a buffer and safeguard to the economic opportunities of our communities, artists have been able to see firsthand the significance of the act as they produce artforms and narratives that often present aspects of their cultural identity that they choose to share with the world. As an artist for most of my life, I would create the elaborate outfits I wear in social and ceremonial settings, often spending hundreds of hours just on the beadwork and feather-work alone. As a participating artist at the Santa Fe Indian Market, my eyes were opened to the economic opportunity that the Native art market offered, as people appreciated my creativity and continuation of art forms that we have often been practicing for generations. Often utilitarian in usage, some everyday forms have evolved into fine art forms in which our artists are able to receive suitable compensation for. Like most perceived opportunities for gain, many of these forms were copied and reproduced, robbed of the native soul and creativity that often accompanies authenticity. I have recently heard first hand from a Navajo Jeweler whose acquired skills began at the age of 12, under the lessons of his silversmith father. He related how he was providing for himself at 14 through his jewelry skills, but given the competition during the 1980's, at the age of 17 he was producing examples for a non-native dealer and working side by side with 40 non-native jewelers to reproduce these items which were then sold as "Native" made. Thankfully, the "truth in advertising" component of the Act protects our artists to some extent.

SWAIA, the non-profit that produces the Santa Fe Indian Market (Indian Market), holds a prestigious and venerated place amongst all Native fine art markets. With humble beginnings in 1922, our market has bolstered and supported generations of Native artists, elevating traditional art forms and in many cases, evolving them. Artists who are able to jury into the competitive market find a venue unlike any other, a place where almost 100,000 people descend upon Santa Fe to experience one of the most beautiful and expressive forms of our cultural identity. In addition to fine art, we partner with the Smithsonian Institution's National Museum of the American Indian to present film and our additional programming includes a Gala auction, art previews, traditional and Couture fashion events, performing arts, and of course, food. Many markets look to our high-level standards requirements as a model for authenticity, and even foreign countries have sent representatives to meet with us in an effort to learn our model for elevating "traditional art and craft forms" to high level fine art.

As thought leaders for a constantly evolving dynamic of how people define "Native" art, our foundation is the artists themselves. We currently accept artists from across all tribes in the United States, and have recently began accepting First Nations artists from Canada. We do require that the participating artists provide proof of enrollment or as Tribal Certified Artisans as per the Act. Year after Year, artists bring their most exciting pieces to Indian Market in the hopes of garnering one of our coveted prize ribbons and accompanying award. These represent achievement of the highest level, not only in the realm of the creative, but in technical mastery and expertise in the form as well. Exquisite jewelry forms, traditional dolls, carved masks, and textiles routinely garner Best in Show next to more recognizable forms of paintings or sculptures. It is amongst these exciting opportunities that the Act has helped to protect, that we have also seen the biggest issues and violations.

Appropriation sees many forms in the Native art community. While there has been a healthy exchange of ideas, songs, dances, and ceremony amongst tribes for generations, there was a protocol and respect associated with an exchange of ideas. Western ideas of property teach differently however. Especially in art. We have most recently seen the appropriation of family designs, often associated with the sacred, taken by fashion designers who claim to want to "honor" or pay homage to native culture. Others simply recognize the popularity of Native design and simply hope to gain. Perhaps the most extreme of these, are those who without enrollment or even descendancy, will appropriate an entire tribal identity in order to gain economically, spiritually, or for some other self-serving reason or status. Our certification process during jurying does eliminate some of these fraudulent artists, but we cannot simply verify with every tribe the validity of their artists. We often rely on our relationship with the Indian Arts and Craft Board to assist us in identifying potential violators. This is a critical component of our market because attendees are assured that what they are seeing and experiencing here is genuine and authentic.

Artists are grateful for the enforcement efforts that have been made to date, but I am sure that the testimony heard today will reflect a desire for increased resources for continued and ongoing enforcement efforts. Just as there is trademark and patent protection for "intellectual property" concepts, so too should there be for artists whose commodity and creation isn't simply art, they are cultural identity concepts. This also places a measure of accountability on tribes themselves. They must have the mechanisms in place to identify their cultural patrimony and verify the validity of their claim. The development of a model mechanism will assist tribes in the creation, tailoring, and evolution necessary to fulfill this accountability. Another mechanism that could be facilitated and presented to tribes for potential adoption would be something to address the Tribal Artisan Certification process for legitimate descendants who simply don't fulfill enrollment requirements for their particular tribe.

Again, I am grateful for the opportunity to present my experiences with the Indian Arts and Crafts Act. While the challenges are many, I do suspect though that moments like this, further definition and clarification, will increase the effectiveness of the Act and its continued protection of Native art forms.

Senator UDALL. Thank you so much, Mr. Maybee. And you've got a real—like all of the witnesses here—they all have real expertise and something to offer here. We hope all of you, as you hear this testimony and then walk away from it, will keep sharing with us your ideas and help us improve on what we have going on right now, which is some good stuff, I think.

Ms. Begay-Foss, love to hear from you. Please proceed.

STATEMENT OF JOYCE BEGAY–FOSS, DIRECTOR, LIVING TRADITIONS EDUCATION CENTER, MUSEUM OF INDIAN ARTS AND CULTURE

Ms. BEGAY-FOSS. Welcome to tribal leadership and officials, Federal and state officials, and other guests.

Thank you, again, Senator Udall and Senator Heinrich and the U.S. Senate Committee on Indian Affairs for scheduling this very important field hearing on the topic of the Indian Arts and Crafts Act.

I am an accomplished weaver for over 40 years, and I have won numerous awards at the Santa Fe Indian Market. And I've also showed at the Eight Northern Pueblo show and San Felipe. So I draw on this expertise as a writer, instructor, and lecturer on traditional Navajo textiles and dyeing techniques. I curated several exhibitions at the Museum of Indian Arts and Culture on Navajo textiles. I've also been involved in addressing issues and concerns about the intellectual and cultural property rights of the Southwest tribes, especially with Diné (Navajo) weavers.

And for many years I've been in contact with local Navajo weaving association groups, such as Ramah Navajo Weavers Association, and Sheep is Life, in Navajo, which is Dibébélin .

My clan is the Nakaidiné (Mexican clan) born for Tachi'ni, (Red Running into the Water People). And I was born in Shiprock, New Mexico. And on my mother's side, that's where I learned weaving from, was from my great aunts who were weavers. So they were like—my mother is in her 80s now, and they were like in their hundreds. I was very fortunate to have that kind of traditional cultural knowledge from them.

And so my aunts lived around Lukachukai, Arizona. And about 30 miles from Lukachukai in Canyon de Chelly, there's an 800-foot tall rock called Spider Rock. So as a child, I was told stories of Spider Woman (Naashjéi Asdz) and said she lived on top of this rock and that she gave our people this gift of weaving.

So for the Navajo people, weaving is not just an art form, the direct connection to our environment and lifeways. Weaving teaches you stamina and perseverance.

And I didn't put some of this earlier stuff in my written testimony, but some of the earliest textiles that we have came from around 1850s and 1880s. This was during the time of Long Walk. So even during that time, our people persevered and carried on that traditional knowledge of weaving.

And today, I feel we're losing that cultural knowledge as well as our language. And it disturbs me that people throughout the world are misappropriating our traditional designs and profiting from it.

Our earliest designs came from our baskets, and then they went into, transitioned into our women dresses, chief blankets, shoulder and child's blankets. These textiles were finally woven from handspun warp and weft woolen yarns. Back then people had their own sheep and goats, and they had to spin it, so they did not have the resource of buying commercial because it was in the 1800s or even earlier.

So colors were limited to natural brown, white, black, and indigo-dyed yarns. In these textiles, patterns were specifically woven a certain color and placement for a reason. However, today the import market has taken some of these very traditional designs and have displaced or rearranged them in knockoffs that I find offensive. We also have regional styles throughout the reservation that have been misappropriated as well. And these styles are Storm Pattern, Ganado, Crystal, Two Grey Hills, Teec Nos Pos, Yei, and Yeibechai, to name a few.

The Two Grey Hills, Ganado, Crystal are actually chapter areas. We have 110 chapter houses on the reservation. And so within these areas, among as weavers, we know, like I come from Shiprock, and Shiprock area, but I know I'm not going to weave a Two Grey Hills rug, out of respect.

So that's why we don't really, like, copyright our designs. It is traditional—Howard brought up it's how we were raised to weave these patterns. So we know what they mean and how the placement is and the colors.

So besides the misappropriation of designs in the import market, Navajo weavers face competition in the lower cost of an import item. Unfortunately, some consumers prefer to buy a cheaper knockoff of a Native American design product. Currently, Navajo knockoffs are being woven in over 15 countries, probably more, including Mexico, Guatemala, Peru, Thailand, Nepal, India, Ukraine, Moldova—which is near Ukraine and Romania—Japan, Egypt and Turkey.

Weavers on the reservation have limited—we have limited venues to sell their rugs. There are few trading posts which will purchase or trade for rugs or blankets. But again, weavers are getting a lower price for their weavings. They can also get their work juried at different art shows in the country. They can gain recognition for their work, and also collectors or buyers can have that consumer confidence in their purchases because the art shows juried work and, you know, they have a screening process.

There are so many issues. So I'm trying to keep it within the five minutes, but there are some other issues to be considered. More education, working with weavers, to have better labeling on their weavings, like saying cultural affiliation. Like we could say it's Navajo or Diné, a description of your weaving patterns, the materials that you use, because we not only have traditional and contemporary, we—I could weave a Navajo rug made out of acrylic yarns.

The Federal law will not protect you as a buyer. It just says it has to be Indian made. It doesn't say it has to be wool. So some buyers might buy a wool rug that might be—have different fibers, and then they get upset, because it's not what they thought they had purchased.

Museums and juried art markets should have how to buy Indian art on their websites. And I'm going to talk to my museum director in my art department to see what we can do to do that.

And then also Indian Arts and Crafts Board, I think they need to hold more workshops nationally on different issues regarding Native American art, not only just for artists but for the general public. I am currently working with the Board on the Navajo weaving brochure, and the museum is providing images of some of our textiles.

So it's very important that we need to educate consumers, and we also need to address, you know, the issue of the importing. Even in the country, though, it's not just imported; it's other designers and other people that are using Native American designs, not just in weaving, but in basketry, in jewelry, pottery, everything.

And there's only 12 states; Alaska, Arizona, California, Colorado, Minnesota, Montana, Nebraska, Nevada, New Mexico, Oklahoma, South Dakota and Texas that have enacted laws prohibiting the misrepresentation of Indian arts and crafts. I think other states need to enact laws as well. Because we have those other issues of the cultural objects and how we're going to prevent people from taking them.

And we need stricter U.S. Custom laws regarding imported non-Native American products coming into the country. And under the former statements earlier, there are obvious—many manufacturers that can be identified.

So thank you again, Senators, and the Committee for allowing me to submit testimony regarding the issues about Navajo weaving.

[The prepared statement of Ms. Begay-Foss follows:]

PREPARED STATEMENT OF JOYCE BEGAY-FOSS, DIRECTOR, LIVING TRADITIONS EDUCATION CENTER, MUSEUM OF INDIAN ARTS AND CULTURE

Thank you to Senator John Hoeven, and the U.S. Senate Committee on Indian Affairs for scheduling a field hearing on the topic of the Indian Arts and Crafts Act.

I am an accomplished weaver for over 40 years and have won numerous awards at the Santa Fe Indian Market, the Eight Northern Pueblos Arts and Crafts Show and the San Felipe Arts and Crafts Show. I draw on this expertise as a writer, instructor and lecturer on traditional Navajo textiles and dyeing techniques. I have curated several exhibitions at the Museum of Indian Arts and Culture on Navajo textiles. I have been involved in addressing issues and concerns of intellectual and cultural property rights of the SW tribes especially with Diné (Navajo) weavers. I am in contact with local Navajo weaving groups such as Ramah Navajo Weavers Association and Sheep is Life (Dibé bé Iiná). *http://navajolifeway.org*

My clan is Nakaiidiné (Mexican Clan) born for Tachii'ni (Red Running into the Water People). I was born in Shiprock, New Mexico and on my mother's side my great aunts were weavers and lived in Lukachukai, Arizona. About 30 miles from Lukachukai in Canyon de Chelly there is an 800 foot tall rock spire (Spider Rock). As a child, I was told stories of Spider Woman (Naashjéii Asdzáá) and that she lives on top of that rock and that she gave the Navajo people the gift of weaving. For the Navajo people weaving is not just an artform but a direct connection to our environment and lifeways. Today I feel we are losing the cultural knowledge as well as our language. It also disturbs me that people throughout the world are misappropriating our traditional designs and profiting from it.

Cultural Misappropriation of design by import market

Our earliest designs came from our baskets and then transitioned into our women's dresses, chief blankets, shoulder and child's blankets. These textiles were finely woven from handspun warp and weft woolen yarns.

Colors were limited to natural brown, white, black and indigo dyed yarns. In these textiles patterns were specifically woven a certain color and placement for a reason. However, today the import market has taken some of these very traditional designs and have displaced or rearranged them in knock-offs that I find offensive. We also have regional styles throughout the reservation that have been misappropriated as well. These styles are: Storm Pattern, Ganado, Crystal, Two Grey Hills, Teec Nos Pos, Yei and Yeibechai to name a few.

Navajo Rug Economy

Besides the misappropriation of designs of the import market Navajo weavers face competition in the lower cost of the imported item. Unfortunately some consumers prefer to buy a cheaper knock-off of a Native American designed product. Currently Navajo knock-offs are being woven in over 15 countries, including Mexico, Guatemala, Peru, Thailand, Nepal, India, the Ukraine, Moldova, Romania, Japan, Egypt and Turkey.

Weavers on the reservation have limited venues to sell their rugs. There are a few trading posts which will purchase or trade for rugs/blankets but again weavers are probably getting a lower price for their weavings. Weavers that can get their work juried at different arts shows in the country can gain recognition for their work and also collectors can have consumer confidence in their purchases.

Other issues to be considered:

- Weavers need to have better labels on their weavings showing: Cultural affiliation (i.e. Navajo/Diné), Description of weaving and materials used.
- Museums and art markets should have: How To Buy Authentic Native American Art on their websites.
- Indian Arts and Crafts Board should be holding workshops nationally on different issues regarding Native American Indian Art for Native Artists as well as the general public. Currently working with Indian Arts And Crafts Board on a Navajo weaving brochure. This brochure in very important to educate consumers and also to address import/knock-off Navajo weavings.
- Only 12 states—Alaska, Arizona, California, Colorado, Minnesota, Montana, Nebraska, Nevada, New Mexico, Oklahoma, South Dakota, and Texas—have enacted laws prohibiting the misrepresentation of Indian arts and crafts. Other states need to enact laws as well.
- Have stricter US custom laws regarding imported non-Native American Indian Art products coming into the country. There are obvious manufacturers that can be identified.

Thank you, Senators and the Committee for allowing me to submit my testimony regarding the issues about Navajo weaving.

Senator UDALL. Thank you so much, Miss Begay-Foss.

And I once again thank all the witnesses. And because you presented such insightful testimony, I have a number of questions here that kind of probe down on what some of you have testified to today.

Mr. Martinez, in your—you've done a lot of law enforcement work. You've worked in various capacities here in New Mexico. You testified that one of the challenges you face in enforcing the IACA is its failure to address importers of Native American-style merchandise.

How would a clear country of origin label help to prosecute violators of the IACA?

Mr. MARTINEZ. Vice Chairman Udall, that is crucial in your consideration from my perspective, because one of the things that you need to show when you're prosecuting these cases is knowledge. And so if you have a clear label of a country of origin on the product itself, that would help the future prosecutors going forward as far as, did the person who's importing the product have knowledge or is the person who's buying the product and then selling it retail have knowledge.

Senator UDALL. And so it sounds like that could be the difference.

Mr. MARTINEZ. Very much so, sir.

Senator UDALL. One of the goals that I have in mind strengthening the IACA so that we dismantle counterfeit operations in their entirety, how could amending the law to include a forfeiture clause help to do that?

Mr. MARTINEZ. Well, through a forfeiture clause, Vice Chairman Udall, it would allow that future prosecutor to seize the money from the operation, seize the proceeds from the operation, and seize any merchandise that was bought from those proceeds.

Senator UDALL. And in a forfeiture, you don't necessarily need a criminal conviction in order to do a forfeiture, is that correct, or would you be recommending the two be combined together?

Mr. MARTINEZ. Well, you have both civil and criminal forfeiture. In this Act, I would, from my personal perspective, I would recommend that you look at a criminal forfeiture, Section 4, amending this Act.

Senator UDALL. Okay, great. Thank you.

Now, you in your testimony talked about, Mr. Martinez, seven recommendations. How would you order those in terms of the most important and the most urgent?

Mr. MARTINEZ. Well, the first recommendation that I would have is—and this goes back to part of your original question—was that there's two places to target; the merchandise being brought into the country and then the point of sale of the merchandise in the country itself.

So I respectfully recommend that you look at adjusting the statute to look at those two points separately. Also, again, just stating what you already mentioned in the question, it's crucial that this statute have—it makes clear that there should be an indelible country of origin marking. Because right now, what the prosecutors need to do is, they need to go a civil—to the Civil Rule, 19 C.F.R. 134.43. But if you can incorporate that requirement in the statute itself, that's going to make a difference.

Also, you mention a forfeiture. That's crucial. 18 U.S.C. § 1956, it's important that you incorporate Section 1159 as a specified unlawful activity. Also, something that is absolutely crucial here is, the U.S. Attorneys' Office, they go after organizations, and one of the sections is 2516, 18 § 2516. That's the authorization for a wiretap statute. And if you can make Section 1159 as an offense for investigation, that would be very important for the fact that again, in going to knowledge, one of the best ways that you prove knowledge is communication.

So if there comes a time in the future that a U.S. Attorneys' Office needs to investigate an investigation, and they're able to prove to the Court that a wiretap is necessary, that would help prove knowledge, that communication.

Senator UDALL. Thank you. And I'm going—I may come back to you in a minute or so.

Mr. Pratt, in your testimony, you gave the real-world example of your brother. A person purchased his work, then replicated it and sold the replicas as authentic. Did your brother file a complaint with the Indian Arts and Crafts Board or did he take legal action on his own?

Mr. PRATT. He took legal action on his own, once he discovered that his work was being duplicated. That rarely happens in the Indian world. They don't have the funds to do those things. And my brother had the funds to do that and stopped this guy from doing that and made him pay royalties and seek what he had left.

Senator UDALL. So he was successful in his legal action, but obviously in a legal action, you have to hire a lawyer, you have to pay the lawyer on an hourly basis, and then you hope to win, but you never know, because there's always two sides of a story in legal cases.

Mr. PRATT. And we see that a lot among Indian artists; that they don't have the assets to do that.

Senator UDALL. Yes.

Mr. PRATT. And if they complain to somebody, they don't have the knowledge to pursue it.

Senator UDALL. What was the role of Federal law enforcement, if any, in your brother's case?

Mr. PRATT. None.

Senator UDALL. None.

Was it reported through various law enforcement channels and outlets?

Mr. PRATT. I think he discovered himself when he saw his work had been duplicated. He originally did it in bronze and the man was duplicating it in silver. When he realized that was his work in silver, he didn't do it, he found out who was selling it under his name as a limited edition. And he filed a charge against him.

Senator UDALL. Now, Mr. Martinez, like any agency, we are oftentimes forced to juggle priorities when we have limited resources. As U.S. Attorney, what was your particular interest in pursuing these counterfeit cases, and would you like to see the current U.S. Attorneys' Office keep on the same path?

Mr. MARTINEZ. Vice Chairman Udall, here in New Mexico, the U.S. Attorneys' Office have great responsibility. We have two national labs. We have military bases. There's immigration issues. There's crime issues. There's a drug epidemic and then what we're talking about today. So with the limited resources, it was important to try to figure out how to prioritize and try to get the limited resources to all these issues that we're talking about.

As stated on your first panel, one of the things that was absolutely crucial was good partnership with the law enforcement agencies and, to the extent possible, with the community when you're doing investigation.

And so what was important in prioritizing is the amount of damage that's occurring in each investigation. The topic that we're talking about today is extremely damaging to the Native American community and with the U.S. Attorneys' Office has a trust responsibility to the Native American community.

And as some of the panelists have already told you, this is damaging to the heritage, it's damaging to the culture, and then as part of that consideration, too, is a large part of the economy in New Mexico is tourism. And it's also damaging there if people can't trust what they're buying.

And just lastly answering your question, it is my hope, and I have to believe that the next U.S. attorney will also keep this as a priority.

Senator UDALL. And I think it's important as a priority, and I will be conveying that to whoever becomes the next U.S. attorney. And I hope that the acting U.S. attorney, which sometimes, you know, the acting U.S. attorneys, if they're listening and understand how important this is, sometimes they serve a—for a matter of months in these kinds of situations. And so they're the top person at the office.

Please go ahead.

Mr. MARTINEZ. Vice Chairman, the current acting U.S. attorney is Jim Tierney. He was first assistant in the office. He has over 33 years of experience in the office. And after having him as my supervisor and having worked with him, I have no doubt that this is a priority for him and for this office.

Senator UDALL. Great. Thank you so much.

Mr. Martinez, when I was attorney general of New Mexico, you may recall that many of the complaints that came into my office were from individuals that felt they were getting a bad deal. So we took action under State law that had been on the books for quite a while. But it seemed to me there should be much more coordination between state, local, and tribal authorities.

As U.S. attorney, did you work with nonFederal authorities on any of these particular cases?

Mr. MARTINEZ. Yes, Vice Chairman Udall. What we tried to do is take the comprehensive approach. The basic is prosecution. But also what we did is, we had a tribal liaison, and we tried to make sure that we were touching base with the tribes as often as possible. We also had listening sessions where we tried to bring all of the tribes together so that they could bring us input on how the U.S. Attorneys' Office was doing—good or bad.

And then also from a regional perspective, we also—and during my last year, we hosted the Four Corners Conference where we brought together the U.S. Attorneys' Office from Utah, Colorado, and Arizona, and the various players in these areas to try to talk as a collective of what we were doing right and what we were doing wrong to be better in the future.

Senator UDALL. And my understanding, when you were the U.S. attorney, you initiated efforts with the leaders of the Indian Nations here in New Mexico and asked their input and how to do better in the job which you were doing, which I'm sure you heard about these issues in that context.

Mr. MARTINEZ. Yes. Vice Chairman Udall, with the limited resources we had, we were trying to get out and talk to the community as much as possible.

Senator UDALL. Do you think it would be possible to have a joint Federal-state-tribal task force to implement a coordinated enforcement response?

Mr. MARTINEZ. Yes, Vice Chairman Udall, to the extent possible. Sometimes you can't do it when you're doing an investigation. But to bring folks together in a collective and try to talk through the issues, one of the most important things is getting people to the table. And that would show that it's a priority.

Senator UDALL. Mr. Maybee, an issue that concerns me is the impact of fake, mass-produced goods that are marketed as authentic Indian arts and crafts on the local economy. As an executive at SWAIA, do you have any experience with Native vendors at Indian Market or elsewhere being impacted by counterfeiters of their work?

Mr. MAYBEE. Absolutely. Obviously, it's disconcerting to hear about an artist going into a local shop and see their hallmark piece of work that they didn't touch. As I talked to other artists. And as an artist myself, you know all the pieces that you've produced in your career, you're very familiar with them and the techniques. And so there is a direct economic impact on the artists when they see counterfeits.

And even then, it's the dynamic between what we do as an organization in terms of educating our visitors and our collectors. We give two licensing agreements to magazines to produce, and give Market publications that are very heavy on educating our collectors and casual visitors, even, as to what's the difference between a thousand dollar squash blossom necklace and maybe a $40 squash blossom necklace that they can find in a shop 20 feet away, often, from artists at Indian Market itself.

And so it's not just the fraudulence. It's the level of standards that are often being seen. In my written testimony, I related an experience of just recently talking to an artist who started his career at the age of 12, and at the age of 14 was using his jewelry skills to provide for himself. But at 17, the competition was so strict, he actually went to work for a dealer who employed 40 additional non-Native artists to produce works that he would produce.

He produced a piece, and the dealer would ask him what he would ask for that and take it to his non-Native jewelers and said, "What can you produce this for?" And often pennies on the dollar in comparison. He only did that for a short time, but it was mainly a matter of survival.

Even today, you can go into the shops in Gallup and see artists who, as a matter of survival, have to undercut each other, because there's 30 other people who will sell—30 other Natives, often—who will sell because of—at a lower price point, these pieces of work, because the dealer will sell them and very unscrupulous and unethical in how they deal with the compensation for these artists.

Senator UDALL. Do you know if Native vendors have been forced to lower prices to compete with the wholesale counterfeits flooding the market elsewhere?

Mr. MAYBEE. Not so much at our market. We've—we have the luxury of having presented authenticity, high-level standards for decades. Generations of artists have been able to utilize the strength of our market and the prestige in order to gain what is fair prices for their work.

But for the rest of the 363 days out of the year, absolutely. If they are struggling to find representation in galleries or find commission work, they have to undersell themselves often, because the dealers know, If I don't get something from this artist, I can go get something similar. And for some, it will be straight counterfeits.

Senator UDALL. Mr. Pratt, I understand you wear multiple hats and have a wealth of experience not only as a master artist but as a former law enforcement officer and the Chairman of the Indian Arts and Crafts Board.

Can you provide some perspective on whether the IACA is serving its intended purpose, and if it's not, ways that we can improve the law.

Mr. PRATT. Well, I think that since 2014, that Indian Arts and Crafts Board and the Indian Arts and Crafts Act has had some success. Prior to that, I think it was very limited because of no enforcement. We had a hard time getting enforcement to enforce laws, because local-state-tribal authorities didn't have the expertise in these specific crimes. And they were limited to just serve jurisdictions.

So they couldn't—many times couldn't cross into other jurisdictions. So I think it was very limited as what we were doing. What we did in 2015, and prior to that, with Fish and Wildlife, that had great impact. I think it opened a lot of people's eyes that things have changed.

And I think I saw that in the past when my brother did that. It made this man change his whole technique about what he was doing. He said, "I've been doing that for 30 years. No one ever stopped me."

He said, "It's a new age."

And I think we see that. Task forces, I think, would be—if we could get people trained, if we could train people at Artesia, train people in Georgia, in the Federal services, to cooperate and realize that this is a tremendous impact on the Indian people and on our economy; that we could train people to pursue these cases.

And the Arts and Crafts Act is instrumental in that, in not only protecting artisans but protecting collectors. And I think that's really important.

Senator UDALL. Thank you. And I think it's important. Like you say, it is a new age. And if people are violating the law, we're going to be coming after them, and they will be brought to justice.

As a Native artist, Mr. Pratt, how are knockoffs impacting your livelihood? Do you believe under-enforcement of the IACA is part of the problem?

Mr. PRATT. I do. I think under-enforcement is part of the problem. People have been doing things for years, you know. You can sell a piece of art, an original painting to someone. And over the years I've seen that thing end up as a print, as a limited edition print, and the artists have nothing to do with it. Artists have never received any kind of royalties at all over those prints and that's just in that.

You see that same thing in sculptures, in duplicating those things. And Indians don't pursue it.

Senator UDALL. Thank you.

Joyce, you're working with the IABC to educate consumers on how to buy authentic Navajo rugs. Why is consumer education so important to preserving the cultural integrity of traditional Navajo weaving?

Ms. BEGAY-FOSS. That's a good question. Well, I think we still have a lot of consumers are not very educated about Navajo weavings, because they're still buying the imported or even knockoffs, as they call them, products. And then even there are other designers—I won't mention their names—but there are companies that produce other products. The designs are taken from Navajo weavings as well.

But the thing that I've been working with Meredith's office, even when I was chair, like, three or four years ago, I brought that issue up to her again. And then I also helped her on a case involving a Navajo weaver trying to sell an imported rug.

But the thing is that consumers look at something and say, "Oh, that's nice." That's a weaving, and they just assume that it was made by a Native person, and it has that Southwest Native design. And then they get home, and they realize, "Oh, my God, this is not even an authentic product."

Even at the museum, we have people come in and bring in—they want to know, "Is this a weaving?" And they ask me. I have visitors that come to the museum. And as a curator and a weaver, I say, "No, this is a Mexican rug or an imported rug. It is not authentic."

And they really get upset. They go, "Oh, my gosh."

And so with the brochure, what we want to do is, like I said in my testimony, we need to get the weavers to say, "Yes, this is my rug. I'm Navajo. This is the style that I weave, whether it's Two Grey Hills, or it's my own personal style. It's made out of wool. It's hand dyed. The warp and weft are wool," or whatever it's made out of.

Because Federal law does not protect the consumer on the materials. And this goes true with all the other art categories, like pottery and jewelry. You know, we have this huge issue with block turquoise. It's not even real turquoise or coral. I don't know, I could go on and on about the jewelry.

But with the weaves, yeah, I think it's very important, because it is affecting the Navajo weavers. So, like, they can barely get 2- or $300 for a small rug today. And that's, like, a couple of hundred hours. And it's, like, barely a dollar an hour. So if you go and you look at, like, some of these imported rugs they sell along the streets, even at, you know, different markets or, you know—what do you call them, flea market type shows, places—you get them for, like, 15, $20, $30. Nothing. To me, I can tell. I'm like, you know, you're getting what you pay for. But, you know, they think they're getting, like, this Native product.

So that's why I think it's important throughout the brochure and to educate the consumer and our Native artists that there is a Federal law, and they have to comply with it. But that's at the Federal level. I think we also need to address state laws, and then I think the tribes—especially Navajo tribe, too—we need to come to the table. And we need to set some, I don't know, laws, or whatever. But I think we need to have some educational things on how to buy products from our communities, whether we have laws or whatever information. Or even if they could have, like, a consumer complaint place, you know, within the different tribal communities and bring up these issues, because we have to start somewhere.

We don't—you know, through all our state and Federal agencies, you know, there's no—there's limited funding. But I think at the grass-roots level in tribal communities, I think we need to watch out for each other, and we need to help. Our people can do that, and that's is how I do it. I talk to the weavers, like Sheep is Life and Ramah Navajo Weavers, and they tell me, you know, "We're having a hard time. We can't make a living."

And, you know, Navajo Nation is remote. There are weavers that live 30, 40 miles from a store. And for them to take their rug and try to sell it to get groceries, you know, it's devastating when you don't have that $50 or $100 to last you a few more days.

So it's economically, and it's culturally, and it's a very—I don't know—distressing topic that we're talking about today.

Senator UDALL. Now, Joyce, what other action can the IACB or Congress take to ensure and build consumer confidence in Indian arts and crafts?

Ms. BEGAY-FOSS. Well, it just comes down to educating people, I think. What are you buying? I mean, you can go buy a diamond ring; you go to a jeweler, "Is that gold, 14 carat gold?"

I think there are not enough questions asked by the consumers when they buy Indian art. They have to look at Federal. Okay. So this person—so the Federal law says it has to be Indian. What does "Indian" mean? I think that definition needs to be elaborated on saying that you need to ask Native American artists—even the word "Indian," people don't like the word "Indian." "Native American," "American Indian." But they need to go by cultural affiliation.

So I can say, "Yeah, made in China," well, where in China is that made? I can't find that as a consumer. But let's say, you know, going back to Indian. If it just said, "Indian made." What the heck does that tell you?

So my responsibility as an artist and as a weaver, I can say, "No, you're buying a Navajo rug from me. It's 30-by-30 inches. It's a saddle blanket. It's made out of churro wool. I have indigo dyes." I sign that, and I give it to my buyer. That's a done deal.

But if the same buyer goes to another weaver and buys it, let's say, not just a Native buyer but a non-Native buyer, because they think it looks Native, and they buy it. "Oh, I thought I bought a Native American product."

I say, "Well, where's your receipt? Where's your proof?"

Has to go to provenance or some kind of a guarantee of authenticity. We have to go to that level, I think, some kind of authenticity certification, receipt from the artist. I think that's going to be our thing that will hold up.

Senator UDALL. Joyce, you testified that for Navajo people, weaving isn't just an art form but a direct connection to your environment and to lifeways. Weaving is also a big part of what you describe as the Navajo rug economy. Can you elaborate on the impact of Navajo rug knockoffs from abroad, on cultural knowledge and the future of traditional Navajo weaving.

Ms. BEGAY-FOSS. Well, first of all, I can say in my testimony, it's very disturbing. And I really get upset about it, because they're misusing our designs. And, in fact, behind you, there are some baskets that are imported on the wall. And those are Navajo baskets, and I really do not like how they misuse even the design of our Navajo culture, because that represents our mountains. That's your life.

All these designs and symbols—especially the traditional designs, not just from our people but throughout our country—our Native people, these early designs mean something to our people. It's beyond—it's sacrilegious, in a way, how they just totally distort and misappropriate the use of the design. And we were taught, growing up, what these designs and patterns meant. So each of the weavers would know what I was—we'd be talking about. It's our connection to the sheep and the horses and the lifeways and, you know, being on the reservation.

Those of us that do—I do natural dyes, so I use rabbit brush. I use sumac and the Native tea. I use indigo, cochineal, and that's connection to those lifeways I'm talking about.

You talk about storm pattern. There's things about cosmology with what the lightning, and the placing even of our four sacred mountains.

I could go on and on. I mean—so to me, these imported designers or people that are taking our designs, and they're abusing—I don't know how to explain it. It's misappropriating, it's abusing our—it goes into the Native American Religious Freedom Act. It's a violation of using our symbol—it's not just a symbol. These things mean something to our people.

I think it's not just the Navajo. It's all of our people throughout the country. And so I think that comes into cultural and intellectual property rights.

Senator UDALL. Joyce, thank you. The fake baskets on display, the point we're making today is, there needs to be better aware- ness. I mean, there's no doubt about that. I think all of our wit- nesses are very much in agreement there. And one of the things that we need is an informed public to know what they're buying. Does the New Mexico Museum of Indian Arts and Culture, which is a very popular tourist destination, does that museum play a role in educating the public on buying authentic Indian arts and crafts? In your opinion, is there any reason to increase public awareness of fake Indian arts and crafts, would be in the best interests of Native artists or the market?

Ms. BEGAY-FOSS. Yes, we do off and on, especially during Indian Market. We will have invited the Indian Arts and Crafts Board. They've done presentations at the museum. We also had intellectual cultural property rights, a person coming in, Deborah Peacock from Albuquerque, she's a lawyer, and she did some presentations.

We try to work with artists, too, and educate them. But like I mentioned in my testimony, I think we need to maybe look at putting that online. And I think all of these things, you have the Hurd Museum—especially museums that have, like, Native art shows. We have Native treasures, too. It's an art show, several hundred artists show it in May. And it's a good venue for artists, too.

So yes, we are trying. Once a month we do have a program called, "Let's Take a Look." But that's when people just bring in things just for us to identify. We don't do appraisals, because you know, we can't do that. We can't do appraisals. But we can tell them if it's authentic or not.

But there is a tremendous need for that. And there are a lot of people that are wanting those type of services or want to learn or read about it. So the public is interested in that.

Senator UDALL. Great. Now, the last couple of questions here for the artists on the panel. Where do you see the future of the Indian arts and crafts business if we don't update the law to include better enforcement? And do you see a role for tribal governments in the future enforcement of the IACA?

Mr. Pratt, why don't you go ahead, and we'll work down the line.

Mr. PRATT. I know Oklahoma has 39 federally recognized tribes; 22 of those tribes have their own law enforcement, and many of their law enforcements are very large. And the other 17 are law enforced by the BIA. And I think that some tribes are making steps to do something to protect their artists. Not all the tribes are doing it.

I think that there should be some kind of training programs to the tribes to make them more aware of the laws and how to protect their own artisans. And I think at that point, an education of the public and collectors is going to be extremely important to know who you buy from. Buy from reputable galleries.

Senator UDALL. Mr. Maybee?

Mr. MAYBEE. Yes. I believe that without increased fine-tuning of the Act itself to strengthen it, not only in terms of enforcement, but also the education on the part of people interested and wanting to engage in Native art. You know, the fraudsters and the dealers of counterfeits, they get savvy. And they are savvy, and they'll increasingly move towards better techniques to defraud consumers.

And we'll hopefully never see the market slide back to what it was back in the '60s and '70s and '80s. So it's going to take some increased efforts on the part of the Act. That doesn't absolve tribes of their own accountability for creating mechanisms to certify unenrolled artisans who have legitimate descendancy.

It is within the tribe's purview to define the membership, but they can go a step further and engage artists who are simply in the business of protecting their art forms and narratives.

A large component of what we do at Indian Market is, we allow for the evolution of art forms. We don't dictate to the artisans what they should or shouldn't create; whether it should be X amount of traditional forms or contemporary forms. That stuff evolves organically. We simply encourage them to keep producing art.

53

Because more often than not, those art forms are direct translations of who they are as people. They engage their lifeways, their traditional and ceremonial narratives. They do a pretty good job of policing themselves and not delve too much into the cultural patrimony. We want to encourage that. We want them to be as expressive as possible and simply be artists and not just Native artists.

The Internet is a very real threat. It is very disheartening to see that not too many prosecutions have occurred over the Internet when all trends indicate that the Internet is going to simply continue to explode exponentially in terms of the amount of commerce that engages in what is often a very anonymous arena.

Dealers can create an eBay website and have it disappear a week later after they have sold significant counterfeits. It makes it very difficult to prosecute some instances where there still is a little bit of anonymity, especially for an unsavvy collector, a person who wants to delve into the area of Indian art.

Senator UDALL. Joyce?

Ms. BEGAY-FOSS. Well, with the Act itself, I would like to see them change the term "Indian" and look more at cultural affiliation for artists. And then also addressing the issue of tribal—what do you call it, like, "blood quantum"?

If there's a way that they can work with tribal leadership, because I know there are families that have—that intermarry or they marry outside. And then—like for me, for example, my grandkids. They're Navajo, but they're not enough Navajo.

So anyway, they come from a strong lineage of ancestral Navajo people, because my great-grandma is Diné, Navajo. Anyway, forget the tribe, forget the government. They're still Diné, no matter what. We are a matriarchal society, so even among our own people and own clans, we do that.

But I think there needs to be something at the tribal level to help some of our other artists, because I think we're going to lose more of those type of artisans in that definition. And we also need to educate the people, artists, and the general public. I mean, it's just ongoing. You have to keep educating people.

I think at the tribal level they need to work more closely at the Federal level and how the Indian Arts and Crafts Board carry out their mission for this big giant import, you know, counterfeit cloud here. We're way over here, and there's this big storm over here. I see this big storm. I don't know how to clear it, to get rid of it, but it's always going to be there, I think.

But we need to work—I think it's a matter of working together as agencies and as people to work on this ongoing issue, because it's not going to go away. I think we really need to just work together.

Senator UDALL. Thank you very much.

Just as a final question to the whole panel or giving you an opportunity to just sum up here, is there anything that you've heard that you want to agree or disagree with, or is there something that we haven't given you the opportunity in terms of asking questions to comment on?

Joyce, why don't you start with you and work to the left.

Ms. BEGAY-FOSS. I think we overall—everyone has some very empowering comments at many different levels. I would like to see more—if we have another hearing on this issue at the tribal level with our leadership and just hear what they have to say and how they can work together with your office at the Federal and then at the state level. And then, you know, look even at revisiting even our state law, and really looking and identifying the, like, the Indian art markets, with Dallin, you know, the Hurd Museum. And, you know, there's other art markets throughout the country, looking at some of the standards, how we can help our consumers.

Because they're the ones that are buying the work. I mean, so you've got to look at, Who are we targeting? And who do we want to listen to us? Who can help us?

So it is just figuring out all the players. I think it is very important to me that myself as a Navajo and member of the Navajo Tribe, that I would like to hear from my leadership on this very issue.

Senator UDALL. Thank you.

Dallin?

Ms. SHAPPERT. So I'm highly encouraged by the efforts that have come from the Federal, state, and even the local level. The City of Santa Fe recently enacted an ordinance that created an Indian Act Zone that mimics the Act in a lot of ways on a state and Federal level with a little bit of an enforcement issue.

They do say that for those vendors who are unscrupulous in their business practice, they can have the potential of having their business license revoked or taken away. It would be nice to see cooperation on the state level if those prosecutions do come through. They can recommend to the City of Santa Fe.

It's elusive, I know. Oftentimes ownership will shift hands from one relative to the next in a span of a day or two. But that does send a message. In terms of the Act itself, one point I wanted to make was, you know, we live in a world where the laws often have to define every aspect. We see it in trademark, in patent law, areas of the law I was not a fan of in law school.

But it was necessary. There's often resistance to defining things to a point, but I think with enough conversation, yes, we can recognize it. It's not enough to simply say, "Oh, this is inspired by" or "I'm paying homage to."

That is very much a loophole to the Indian Arts and Crafts Act. So if we can continue to work towards those definitions of who is an Indian, what does it mean to be a Native artisan or to create Native art, I think we still need to move forward.

Senator UDALL. Thank you.

Harvey?

Mr. PRATT. I think that we need to move towards training and education. Training of law enforcement, workshops with galleries, with the tribes, make them more knowledgeable of what their rights are and what they can expect if they discover something wrong, who they can go to, to effect a result; whether it be on a Federal level or state level, tribal level. A lot of states have reservations. Oklahoma does not have a reservation. We have trust lands, allotted lands, and tribal lands. And allotted land could be in the house next door to you. It would be tribal land and have no jurisdiction there.

So I think that we need to educate collectors and the public and artisans and tribes about what they can expect.

Senator UDALL. Thanks.

Damon?

Mr. MARTINEZ. Senator, I would ask that in addition to revising the statute, that you would also consider respectively contacting the U.S. Department of Homeland Security, specifically the U.S. Customs and Border Patrol, CBP, because when they're doing the inspections at the port, they need to know about the C.F.R. that's currently in place. And if they come across anything that isn't marked, that they either flag it or seize it.

And so that's going to be the first line of defense right there. And thank you for this opportunity to speak to you today.

Senator UDALL. Great. Thank you so much. And I just really want to thank this panel—the previous panel—but in particular this panel that I think brought really insightful testimony to what the harm is, what we're talking about here. And I think all of us, my staff here, we've learned a lot, and so we really appreciate you sharing with us and giving these examples and taking your time to do that.

Since there are no more questions for today, I would like to remind folks that senators that are on this Committee, they also submit follow-up written questions to you for the record. You may get questions from the Chairman. Senator Hoeven really appreciates that the Chairman sent his top person out here, and I know that he may visit us in the future, and I may visit him in North Dakota.

He's been a great chairman of the Senate Indian Affairs Committee. He's been very interested in the issues that we've talked about today. And I really hope—he's got many tribes in North Dakota. I hope I'll have an opportunity to visit Senator Hoeven there. And so I thank him very much.

The hearing record will be open for two weeks. I thank the witnesses again for their time and testimony. I just want to say a word about staff. And thank you, Senator, for being here, former Senator Ben Nighthorse Campbell. He's been here the whole time listening and hearing all of this.

You know, one of the things that I've learned being a senator is, to be a good senator, you've got to have a great staff. And we've had a great staff effort in this entire operation here. We have the Senate Indian Affairs Committee staff here. Jennifer Romero and Anthony Sedillo, both of them are native New Mexicans.

We also have Mike Andrews and Holmes Whalen from Senator Hoeven's staff. Also, the personal staff of my office that's helped with all of the organization here; Josh Sanchez, Greg Bloom, my State director, Alex Jordan, Ned Adrian, Zoey Wilson-Meyer, and Cal Curlen.

So we appreciate all of the things that they've done, and I'm going to tap the gavel, but I want you to just recognize we're also going to recognize—is Jude still here for the closing prayer?

Okay, terrific.

Senator Campbell, did you—you're going to—you want a closing comment, a quick one?

Senator CAMPBELL. Yes.

Senator UDALL. Please come on up. I call him Senator Campbell, you don't know I say former senator.

The tradition with senators is, Once a senator, always a senator. So Senator Campbell, give us your closing.

Senator CAMPBELL. The only advantage of being an ex is, you don't get as much hate mail.

I really haven't been to a hearing for a long time. I was really interested in the testimony. I would mention even when I was the chairman, there is always budget constraints.

Under the present, current budget of President Trump, there's going to be a 30 percent cut in the Interior's funds. Part of that money comes out of the Indian Arts and Crafts Board. Even when I was active in the Senate, they were always ramming against the edge trying to do more with less. They're going to need a champion this year, and I know you're going to be that champion, Mr. Chairman.

This was really interesting to me because about three weeks from now, as Chairman Maybee will tell you, there will be over 100,000 people in this town, and the vast majority are wonderful, caring, loving people that are going to spend a lot of money, visit with Native people, support Native people, and so on.

But in that 100,000 crowd, just like any crowd of 100,000, there's going to be a couple of rats. And it's always been that way with any major group. But in this case, they will be around photographing or copying right through your glass cases of the artist. And a month later, you'll see those in a magazine made in China.

That actually happened to me with a necklace I made one time years ago. In fact, I think it made it into Indian Market that year. And within a year later, I saw it in a magazine which comes from China. Well, where does that leave an individual craftsman? It leaves you out in the cold. You don't have the resources to sue them in an international court.

So you just kinda wave, oh, you've been ripped off, and you can't do anything about it. So as you dream up the new revisions of the bill, Mr. Chairman, if you can also look at how we—maybe not protect, maybe that's not a good word—but educate Native people and how they can record their work, document their work, and protect themselves, either through going through a patent office registering the name as a copyrighted name or at least on their designs, or something of that nature. Because clearly, there's a big deficit between how they make something and how they protect it from being plagiarized.

Thank you so much for this hearing, and thank you for inviting the old man back.

Senator UDALL. Thank you for the closing comments. Really appreciate that. I'm going to adjourn. But as soon as we adjourn, we're also going to have Jude up here and recognize him. He's from the Santa Clara Pueblo to offer the closing prayer. So the hearing is adjourned.

And Jude, why don't you come up and give us a closing prayer.

[Closing prayer recited.]

[Whereupon, at 1:13 p.m, the Committee was adjourned.]

A P P E N D I X

PREPARED STATEMENT OF JOHN MOLLOY, PRESIDENT, ATADA [1]

ATADA is an international organization honoring the artistic vision of indigenous people. ATADA represents professional dealers of historic and contemporary tribal art from around the world. We support the lawful circulation, trade, collection, preservation, appreciation, and study of art and artifacts from diverse cultures.

Our objectives are to promote ethical and professional conduct among art dealers, to encourage the responsible collecting, research, and study of tribal arts and culture, and to educate the public in the contribution of tribal cultures to the wealth of human experience.

As a condition of membership, ATADA members guarantee the authenticity of all objects that they offer for sale.

ATADA is deeply concerned by the misrepresentation and mislabeling of Native American, Native Alaskan, and Native Hawaiian works of art and craft. Misrepresentation deceives individual consumers and the public. When misrepresentation occurs, it also damages the reputation of the art trade as a whole. Bad business practices by a few bad apples can negatively impact many honest traders, Native artisans, art dealers, and other important commercial interests. There is a trickle-down effect to all legislation affecting Indian arts and crafts which impacts much larger constituencies and business interests, whether they are those of workers in the cultural tourism industry, or the diverse businesses that depend upon tourism, especially in the Southwestern region.

It is early in the legislative process and no specific amendments to the Indian Arts and Crafts Act have yet been proposed. Without having actual proposed amendments to respond to, ATADA states that it supports in principle the amending of the Indian Arts and Crafts Act to provide greater protections for consumers and the public, Native artists, and the legitimate art trade. However, ATADA notes that currently, prosecutors and tribal plaintiffs have excellent tools to combat fraud and misrepresentation in domestic matters, and to require proper, indelible labeling in foreign imports. The problem is not that stronger laws are needed; resolution requires more and stronger enforcement of existing laws, and funding to ensure that tribes are equipped to fight using the legal tools already to hand.

Testimony at the hearing by Damon Martinez, former U.S. Attorney for New Mexico, pointed out the need to distinguish between (1) steps to improve the U.S. Customs marking requirements for imports to ensure that the items are not later misrepresented, and (2) steps to halt and penalize misrepresentation and other unfair business practices in the U.S.

Proper Marking On Imported Goods

Proper marking is a key issue, as has been made clear by the descriptions at the hearing of arrests and prosecutions of large scale wholesalers alleged to have imported copies of Native American jewelry from the Philippines. Continuing investigations and prosecutions of individuals and corporate entities found to be engaged in wrongful wholesale imports appears to be working very well and will put a significant dent in any fraudulent activity, if it does not end it altogether.

ATADA recognizes the inherent difficulties in indelibly marking very small objects (such as certain jewelry items) with the country of origin. Tagging protocols should not interfere with the lawful importation and sale of properly identified items. However, packaging and other options may provide a more flexible mechanism to make

---

[1] ATADA is a professional organization established in 1988 in order to set ethical and professional standards for the art trade and to provide education for the public. ATADA membership has grown to include hundreds of antique and contemporary Native American and ethnographic art dealers and collectors, art appraisers, and a strong representation of museums and public charities across the U.S., dedicated to the promotion, study and exhibition of Native American history and culture. *www.atada.org.* email director@atada.org, PO Box 45628, Rio Rancho, NM 87174.

clear the origin of a very small object. Larger items could reasonably be indelibly marked through a variety of means.

If millions of dollars' worth of fraudulently imported jewelry has been seized, as stated at the hearing, the federal government ought to do its best to fill this gap in inventory and at the same time, encourage economic development that would benefit tribal artists. One wonders whether the National Park Service could work with the Indian Arts and Crafts Board or with tribal communities to bring more authentic Native American arts and crafts into the federal parks' concessions, especially in Indian Country, and make authenticity a primary selling point.

Native artists receive recognition for the authenticity of their work when it is sold in the U.S. or elsewhere is another important task, in which enforcement of consumer protection laws is key. Marking options that would distinguish authentic contemporary Native American artworks and crafts could facilitate enforcement.

Antique items cannot easily be marked without damaging the integrity of the object. No rules requiring marking should be employed for antique items. In this situation, consumers should be able to rely of a written receipt and guarantee that items are as represented; guaranteeing authenticity is mandatory for ATADA members already.

Authenticity and Consumer Rights Under State Law

ATADA strongly supports strengthened scrutiny of items offered for sale to the public as Native American and rigorous enforcement of consumer protections. We note that in New Mexico (and in several other states) state consumer protection laws can be a significant deterrent to bad businesses. Government should provide flexibility under the Indian Arts and Crafts Act for the Indian Arts and Crafts Board to provide advice and support to plaintiffs regarding state laws as well. This could enable cases to be brought on behalf of artisans and consumers at a lower cost, and to reap greater damages from violators.

For example, New Mexico's Indian Arts and Crafts Sales Act, NMSA 1978 § 30–33–7 makes it unlawful to barter, trade, sell, or offer for sale or trade any article represented as produced by an Indian unless the article is produced, designed, or created by the labor or workmanship of an Indian. NMSA 30–33–10 grants a private right of action to all consumers, and NMSA 1978 30- 33–6 establishes a duty on the part of the seller to enquire whether an item is authentically Indian and a duty to correctly label the item at the point of sale.

Misrepresenting an item as Native American when it is not is a deceptive trade practice under NMSA 1978 § 57–12–2.D(4), which prohibits using deceptive representations or designations of geographic origin in connection with goods and services. Willful violation of the standards creates liability for sellers of non-Indian goods under New Mexico laws of triple actual damages or $300.00, whichever is greater, under New Mexico's Unfair Practices Act, NMSA 1978 57–12–10.B.

Attorney fees for plaintiffs are more easily available under both New Mexico's Unfair Practices Act (NMSA 1978 § 57–12–10.B) and the Indian Arts and Crafts Sales Act , NMSA 1978 § 30- 33–1, both of which provide that on showing of a violation, the court must award attorney fees and costs.

Copyright and Trademark

Copyright and trademark were also briefly discussed at the hearing. Much of the discussion surrounding misrepresentation of Indian art at the hearing was in regard to wholesale importation of jewelry and textiles in imitation of Native American artistic styles. A "style" cannot be copyrighted, and even specific designs that are considered "traditional" were never copyrighted and are not eligible to be copyrighted now under the U.S. Copyright Act of 1976 (Public Law 94–553, October 19, 1976).

Nonetheless, the specific creations of contemporary jewelers and weavers may be copyrighted, if they are deemed "original" under the law and meet other copyright requirements. While acknowledging that federal trademarks can be expensive to acquire, ATADA suggests that tribal organizations might consider establishing tribal trademarks that would serve as both an identifying mark and a marketing vehicle. ATADA supports federal funding to facilitate economic development programs within the tribes to provide education and assistance in trademark and copyright for tribal artists and artisans through the Indian Arts and Crafts Board, tribal heritage offices or tribal governments.

Conclusion

ATADA urges the Senate Committee on Indian Affairs to consult with tribal government and economic development offices in order to determine the most direct and effective means of establishing authenticity for artworks in the market. The most successful measures will be those that boost consumer confidence and encourage the artists of the Native American community to continue to produce the out-

59

standing works of art that represent Native American creativity and skill and that have come to symbolize the wonderfully diverse and unique Southwestern culture. ATADA looks forward to further discussions with the Senate Committee on Indian Affairs on this and all other legislation affecting the interests of the trade in contemporary and antique Indian art.

———

PREPARED STATEMENT OF KATHY M'CLOSKEY, PH.D., ADJUNCT ASSOCIATE PROFESSOR/FREELANCE CURATOR, DEPARTMENT OF SOCIOLOGY, ANTHROPOLOGY AND CRIMINOLOGY, UNIVERSITY OF WINDSOR

I am writing as a U. S. citizen and anthropologist who has researched how the escalation of knockoffs of Navajo weaving designs is increasingly impoverishing reservation weavers. I authored *Swept Under the Rug: A Hidden History of Navajo Weaving,* UNM Press 2002/2008, and served as research director of the PBS documentary "Weaving Worlds," directed by Navajo Bennie Klain 2008. Both the book and the film provide evidence of the destructive effects that knockoffs have had on diminishing demand for authentic creations.

In her eloquent testimony Joyce Begay-Foss noted that "we can't make a living," and she mentioned how appropriation of Navajo designs is in violation of the Native American Religious Freedom Act. It is also in violation of Articles 11, 20, and 31, of UNDRIP, the UN Declaration on the Rights of Indigenous Peoples. The articles stress the right of Indigenous Peoples "to maintain, control, protect and develop their heritage, traditional knowledge and expressions. . . [including] designs, and the intellectual property over traditional cultural expressions." Part II of Article 11 stipulates that states shall "provide redress, including restitution with respect to their cultural, intellectual, religious and spiritual property taken without their free, prior and informed consent."

It is very troubling that the magnitude of the problem has continued to increase, even though the Act was significantly strengthened within the past two decades. There is no question that Internet sales have grown exponentially, and pose a major threat due to the impersonal nature of transactions that can occur globally within a fraction of a second. Even if Al-Zuni is shut down in the U. S., it could continue to market knock-offs in any other country in the world. I doubt there is anything that the government can do about such sales.

Although the recent hearing contained compelling testimony from eight presenters, the root of the problem concerns the lack of protection for Native American communal property rights, because the government placed designs in the public domain over a century ago. Regardless of how much 'truth in advertising' exists, the exponential increase in knock-off sales, allowable under free enterprise, increasingly impoverishes Native American households. For example, the Pendleton Company website advertises classic Navajo rug designs woven by Zapotec weavers living in Mexico. El Paso Saddle Blanket Company of Texas, continues to wholesale thousands of "trading post rugs" woven in Eastern Europe. Both companies comply with the IACB Act.

In her testimony Meredith Stanton noted that the Board has prosecuted 22 cases successfully over the past two decades. Although each successful prosecution is a victory, Native American artisans continue to endure appropriation of their designs from unscrupulous entrepreneurs. In 2006 two friends were browsing shops in Santa Fe located on the Plaza. They were admiring a beautiful Navajo rug that had the weaver's photo attached. When one of the staff noted their interest, he said that if they couldn't afford a genuine rug, Packards would have it copied for a much cheaper price! These are just three examples of legitimate companies that practice "truth in advertising." I also know several weavers who have experienced theft of their designs.

The recent hearing seeks to modernize and improve the IACA. It is evident from the testimony that an increase in the budget will be necessary if government agencies can root out and escalate prosecution of guilty parties. Perhaps the IACB could also review how Australia, New Zealand, and Canada to some extent offer design protection for their Indigenous Peoples. I have attached three publications which address this serious issue.

Please don't hesitate to contact me if I can be of assistance. *

———

* The article *Diasporas of and by Design, Historicizing the Growing Impoverishment of Native American Artisans* by Kathy M'Closkey [Anthropology News November 2013] has been retained in the Committee files.

Mr. Chairman, Members of the Committee, Tribal Leaders and Guests:

On behalf of the Pueblo of Acoma ("Pueblo" or "Acoma"), we are deeply appreciative of the time taken by the Committee and your staff to travel to Santa Fe in order to devote your attention examining the state of the Indian Arts and Crafts Act.

The Indian Arts and Crafts Act is an important safeguard to ensure the integrity of American Indian Art and the cultural sovereignty of our tribes and our artists. Therefore, we are eager to share our experiences with the limits of the Indian Arts and Crafts Act as it is tested against new and unforeseen challenges.

The Pueblo of Acoma, like many pueblos, is world renowned for its pottery. We are proud to support Acoma's masterful potters, who maintain a tradition we have known since time immemorial in gathering, shaping, and forming clay into beautifully shaped pots. The intricate designs that carefully adorn these potteries have been handed down from generations, many having specific cultural meanings or having been used by specific families to be passed down through new generations of potters. The culmination of the time, physical effort, and prayers recited, as these potteries come to life, results in beautiful works of art that are distinct in shape and design; recognizable against other pueblos, and a unique expression of Acoma culture.

As a result, Acoma pottery is highly sought after by collectors and the general public alike. Acoma pottery adorns many homes, collections, galleries, and museums. Even an Acoma pot by the late Lucy Lewis, a master Acoma potter and matriarch of Pueblo pottery, sat in the Oval Office of Former President Barack Obama, on loan from the National Museum of the American Indian. Acoma is proud to share our art as an expression of our cultural heritage with the world.

However, the Pueblo of Acoma is very particular in its statement: "our cultural heritage;" and insists on the right to dictate who may use our name, "Acoma" and designs. We believe this stance aligns with the spirit of the Indian Arts and Crafts Act, and its original intention of promoting tribal art and protecting tribal artisans.

Therefore, it was extremely troubling for the Pueblo of Acoma when we learned of the appropriation of Acoma's name and designs by companies and merchants seeking to capitalize on Acoma's culture and artists. Two glaring examples that came to the Pueblo's attention were the creation of an Acoma themed clothing line by the designer Tory Burch, and the sale of Acoma themed home and bath products by the company Avanti. Both were being sold at major retailers across the country. Acoma learned of each example after the products were discovered for sale by Acoma members, who immediately recognized the familiar Acoma designs both online and in retail stores[1]. For Tory Burch, the Pueblo unfortunately learned after the collection line had made its run in retail stores; undoubtedly resulting in thousands of dollars made on the use of Acoma's name and pottery designs. For Avanti, the Pueblo learned of the active sale of linen and ceramic products adopting Acoma's name and pottery designs while they were being actively sold in multiple major retail stores; similar to Tory Burch, that likely resulted in thousands of dollars in sales. Both companies never asked permission from the Pueblo of Acoma for usage of its name, or its cultural designs that are the creation of our ancestors and present artists.

Ultimately, the Pueblo of Acoma made the difficult decision to not pursue legal action to halt the usage of its name and its designs. In the Pueblo's analysis of each incident, the Pueblo was unclear as to how such claims would ultimately hold up in federal court. In large part, the federal case, *Navajo Nation v. Urban Outfitters*, played a significant role in the analysis of a similar lawsuit. Unfortunately, for the Pueblo, *Navajo Nation* was settled, but did offer insight in the limits the Pueblo might face if it made a similar claim. In *Navajo Nation*, the New Mexico federal district court dismissed several of Navajo Nation's causes of action, including claims about the usage of the name "Navajo," as the court did not agree the name met the burden of rising to a national trademark. Arguably, the Navajo Nation, in its case, was in a better position than Acoma as the Navajo Nation holds several trademarks

---

[1] See Attachment 1 for photos.

incorporating its name, which Acoma does not. The Pueblo of Acoma was deterred from seeking relief after seeing the major hurdles, and costly litigation that faced Navajo Nation.

The cultural appropriation faced by the Pueblo of Acoma, and the Navajo Nation, is a new issue not contemplated by the Indian Arts and Crafts Act. Certainly, the rapidly shifting intellectual property frameworks have far outpaced the Indian Arts and Crafts Act in being able to respond to the appropriation and use of tribal names and designs. Although, the appropriation of names and designs for "inspired" products is not exactly the same as the counterfeiting that the Indian Arts and Crafts Act most directly deters; the appropriation of tribal names, design, and art ultimately harms the very people the Act seeks to protect. It is clear to the Pueblo of Acoma, that the Indian Arts and Crafts Act needs to be revisited to respond to these new issues, and workarounds that companies have developed to profit off of our cultural art and heritage.

Attachment 1

A.) Tory Burch Product Examples:

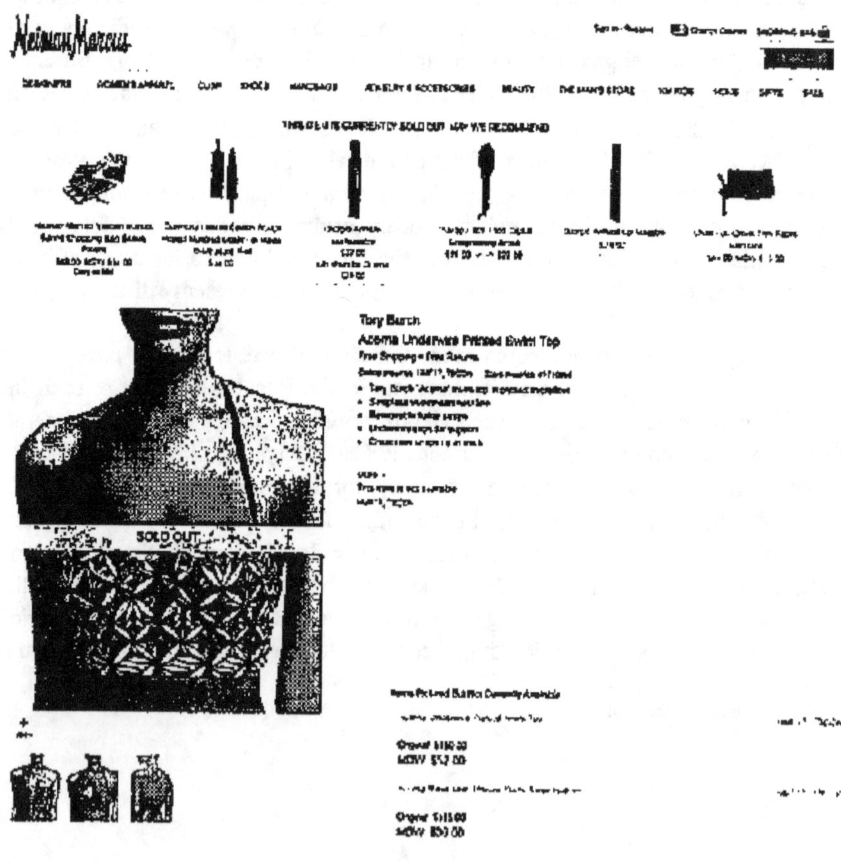

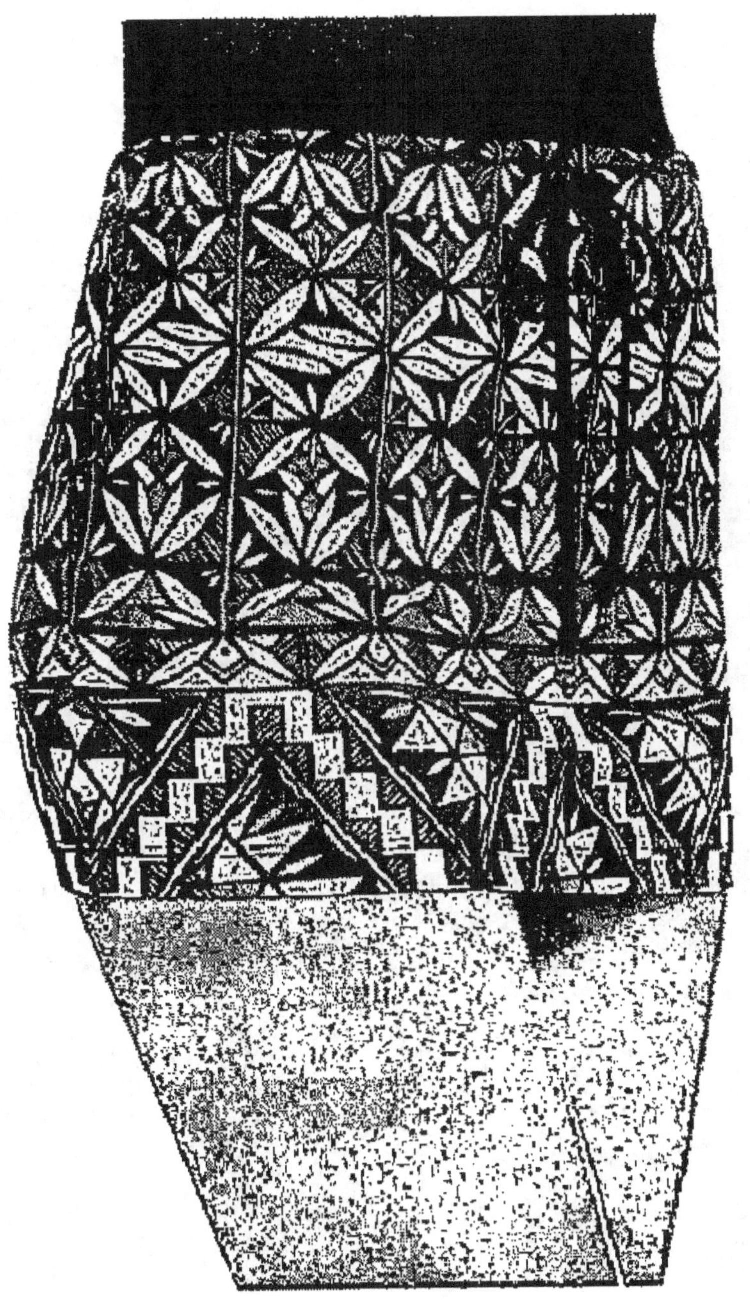

B.) Avanti Product Examples:

PREPARED STATEMENT OF ROY MONTIBON, CEO, MONTIBON PROVENANCE
INTERNATIONAL, INC.

Dear Senator Udall, Senator Heinrich and the Senate Committee on Indian Affairs,

I attended the Oversight Field Hearing on Modernizing the Indian Arts and Crafts Act in Santa Fe on July 7th, 2017. I was impressed with the quality of the testimony given and the sincerity of the Senators present. Senator Ben Nighthorse Campbell's comments were particularly interesting.

It is concerning that the problem of fraud in the world of Native American arts is now international in scope. Native Americans have been exploited and harmed enough. As an American citizen, I am outraged that nameless, faceless con-artists in other countries are exploiting Native American artists. As a nation we must do as much as we can to end the fraud that is rampant here in New Mexico, across the U.S. and around the globe.

I understand that U.S. Fish and Wildlife Service, the FBI and other participating Federal agencies have their hands full with these complex undercover investigations. The Indian Arts and Crafts Act definitely needs to be updated to give it more teeth—more legal tools for law enforcement and prosecutors to leverage when going after fraudsters (including asset forfeiture, etc.)

However, I'd like to bring to the attention of the Senate Committee that there are also new technical tools and processes that can also be brought to bear on this problem.

Our New Mexico tech startup, Montibon Provenance International (MPI) protects art, antiquities and cultural artifacts against forgery, fraud, theft, and counterfeit documentation (chain-ofcustody) by utilizing proprietary object identification technologies and chain-of-custody processes.

MPI has been involved in R&D with nanotechnology scientists at a private lab in Albuquerque and physicists at Los Alamos National Labs to effectively solve each of these problems, (including cyber-security and long-term data archiving innovations). In lab testing to date, MPI solutions have proven to be effective. MPI has been awarded two NMSBA LANL research grants; have received three small NSF-related grants through the NMFAST program coordinated through the Arrowhead Center at NMSU; and are currently applying for the NSF I-Corps pre-SBIR program.

As you are aware, standard methods of identifying and authenticating art objects to protect and track them over time present problems for artists, collectors, museums and law enforcement.

MPI is particularly focused on working to solve the problem of fraud in the Native American art market as Native artists are particularly vulnerable to such fraud. Unlike artists and collectors in the general contemporary art market, many Native artists do not have the personal financial wherewithal to seek justice through civil actions. In addition, the frauds against Native artists go beyond purely financial crimes and are actually crimes against American Indian culture, traditions and sovereignty, and thus, are particularly egregious.

We would love to present our technological innovations to the Senate Committee as we feel that our New Mexico-developed solutions can make significant contributions as useful tools for law enforcement and prosecutors in criminal cases to: reduce the complexity and ambiguity of legal cases; increase the recoverability of stolen tribal artifacts; reduce the amount of counterfeit objects in circulation; and add weight to IP-related cases.

JOINT PREPARED STATEMENT OF HON. JAMES WRIGHT, CHIEF, MA-CHIS LOWER CREEK INDIAN TRIBE AND NANCY CARNLEY, VICE CHIEF

We appreciate the opportunity to testify regarding the Modernizing of the Indian Arts and Crafts Act.

The Ma-Chis Lower Creek Indian Tribe of Alabama is a State Recognized Tribe by the State of Alabama.

The Ma-Chis Lower Creek Indian Tribe of Alabama supports the modernizing of the Indian Arts and Crafts Law and supports strengthening the ability to enforce this Act as it should be. The Ma-Chis Lower Creek Indian Tribe of Alabama works to make sure that this Law is adhered. This Tribe has requested and continues to request the publication regarding the Indian Arts and Craft Law (from the Department of Interior) to disseminate to every tribal citizen, pow wow committee member, vendor, demonstrator, that participates at the Ma-Chis Lower Creek Indian Tribe of Alabama. The Pow Wow Chairman verifies that each vendor is a citizen of a state or federal tribe if a vendor is not their booth has a sign placed in front Non-Native Made.

I do not believe that the definition of who an Indian artisan is should be changed. It says quite clearly that "Indian is defined as a member of a federally or officially State recognized Tribe, or a certified Indian artisan"; and the definition of Indian Tribe as "Any federally recognized Indian Tribe, Band, Nation, Alaska. . ." and "Any Indian group that has been formally recognized as an Indian Tribe by a State Legislature, a State Commission, or another similar organization. . .".

There will always be people who will try to circumvent the law. These people could be impersonating a federally-recognized Indian, a state-recognized Indian, or a certified Indian artisan. To ignore state-recognized tribes simply to make things easier is not the answer. Again, the Ma-Chis Lower Creek Indian Tribe of Alabama will continue in our endeavors to enforce the Indian Arts and Crafts Act.

Thank you for this opportunity to share the concerns of the Ma-Chis Lower Creek Indian Tribe of Alabama Tribal people.

———

PREPARED STATEMENT OF AIDEN SHORTCLOUD, TRIBAL ARTIST, UNITED CHEROKEE ANIYUNWIYA NATION (UCAN)

To the Vice Chairman Udall and Senator Heinric and all others who attended the field hearing last Friday. I am a recognized tribal artist of the United Cherokee Aniyunwiya Nation (UCAN) My relatives can be found on the Cherokee Miller Rolls and the Henderson Rolls. Both are federal rolls that are dismissed by the Cherokee Nation of Oklahoma as well as the Eastern Band Cherokee of North Carolina. I am therefore a State Recognized artist. My tribe requires documentation to a direct relative on any of the Cherokee Federal Rolls. There are 15 Cherokee rolls. The Federally recognized tribes only take 3 of these. Meaning for me my family is on the Miller roll which after 1923 was retaken as the final Baker Roll of Eastern Band Cherokee, all others before it no longer qualifies. My tribe's standards are the same as Cherokee Nation, except they take all 15 rolls, not just one.

To be clear I am writing on behalf of myself and not representing my nation or any other organization to whom I coordinate with. I have been an artist since I was 8 years old. I make drums, I dance, I tell stories. I have a few art pieces here and there that have made it into museums. I make quality art that has been used by the History Channel, National Geographic and many other organizations.

As Native people we rely on the sale of our art as a valuable source of income and of course a way to keep our traditions strong. Authentic art and authentic materials are becoming harder and harder to find. For example: The quahog shell that we use to make wampum beads from is no longer getting to a dark purple. The oceans are becoming more and more polluted. The Beautiful pink shell beads the Shoshone Bannock people in Idaho use for their loop necklaces are now endangered and can not be found. With the threats of deforestation and more and more regulations towards what can and can not be sold are causing artists to have to use plastics and fake materials. This severely lowers the quality of art. The amount of people still producing Brain tan leather at an affordable price are disappearing. On my trip to New Mexico this spring I was disappointed to find that the tribal silver artists are no longer making the beautiful turquoise items that used to be everywhere in my youth. The silverwork is plain, common looking. . . No Sterling feathers swirling around stones. . . Plain. . . The truth of the matter is we are also fighting larger pictures of destruction from overharvesting that is zapping our materials to make art. The laws in states allowing us to harvest the items needed to make this art are becoming more and more strict.

There is no exemption for these products made unless you are a member of an Alaskan tribe. For example. I live in Idaho, here we are allowed the harvest of black bear. Two bears a year per person. We hunt in the fall for the fat, we use it to make an arthritis paste, we use it for soap, we use it for waterproofing, the list goes on. We hunt in the spring because the meat is also leaner at this time. We don't hunt for the fur, so we have always sold it along with the claws. The money from this is distributed to my business, then to my tribe, then to local organizations, then to prison facility native programs and then to national organizations to help everyone to continue our strong culture. I sell claws and hides to other natives to make their art as well. Let's face it, it is hard to make a sterling silver bear claw pendant, without a bear claw. . . . .

However, now many states don't allow you to sell these products. This has lead to large websites such as *www.Etsy.com* to allow only Alaskan natives to sell their bear products (due to the exemptions in the Endangered Species act stated earlier for native made art) Yet there are no exemptions for other tribal artists who hunt and fish just as traditionally. This has lead to us throwing away bear hides, if I can't sell them I can' afford to make my art. It costs me $400 to tan a bear hide so that I can paint it and turn it into a robe that I might be able to sell for $600. So now, the art is dying. There are people who want these items to purchase to support me and my tribe, but due to laws they can not purchase and I can not sell. It creates a terrible waste for something that can be used and made into authentic art.

I propose that the exemptions for Alaskan and Inuit artists also extend to any person enrolled in a state of federally recognized tribe. Because this art is preserving our art and culture it's being purchased for spiritual use and it is being hunted for meat as discussed in our sovereign treaty rights. I am not suggesting being able to sell migratory bird items in any way, but to allow tribal artists to use materials such as bear claws that are considered endangered in one state but are being harvested legally and made into authentic art by a native person.

Another point I would like to bring up is websites such as *www.etsy.com* just spend five minutes on there and you will see no enforcement of the arts and crafts act. Vintage Chinese made imports line the top posts where as actual artists have little to no representation. *www.ebay.com* enforces this by requiring us to put out name and tribal affiliation. But still people list these fake items and confuse buyers. It is discouraging to have to look for 30 minutes to find maybe one or two pieces of native art that is genuine. I have written Etsy and all e-mails have been ignored, I have flagged listings and they remain up. I have reported Etsy to the IACA as well as the BIA and nothing has come of it. The fake fashion headdress remains. What if the site required verification or a tribal ID on file with the artist of a state or federal tribe? Disclosing my name and tribal status before the purchase of an item allows people to steal my name online. I always send a certificate of authenticity with the piece but it is very scary having that information out there for someone to take.

Lastly in November 2016 Oklahoma passed a law banning my art from being considered Native American made because I am a member of a state recognized tribe.

Oklahoma state also expanded the law to cover storytelling and any visual demonstration. This is in direct violation under the federal arts and craft act. As we saw with marriage equality state laws can not trump federal law. My family lives in Ardmore Oklahoma. We have lived between Ardmore and Rusk county for the past 6 generations. . . This severely effects me when I go home to visit my dad. I refuse to sell in that state, and it causes resentment towards the federal tribes. I am fortunate enough to live in Idaho where my art is still protected. However, this is very sad. Not only has it silenced my art, I can not competitively dance in that state. If I am paid for any activity where I state that I am a tribal member/ Native American I am in violation of state law but well within rights granted by Federal law. . . This means if I enter a competition pow wow dance and say I'm Cherokee I get a fine. Because I am not a member of a federal tribe there. It is a hidden agenda to make sure that only Federal tribal people can participate in cul- tural events and receive compensation. To me that just means they want a monop- oly on the Arts and Crafts. Let's not forget some tribes have lost their federal rec- ognition and are now State recognized. Are they any less native? Oklahoma has in- creasingly become more and more exclusive. The state recognized tribes have been in existence since before 1990. The Powhatan tribes (many are state recognized) have always existed and are still state recognized. The Lumbee tribe is a great ex- ample of a state recognized tribe. They have treaties going back to pre 1900 and are STILL fighting for federal recognition. I would like to remind everyone that this law was created to protect Authentic handmade Native American Art from corpora- tions and cheap fake imports. . . It wasn't designed to tear each other apart. To put tribal people against one another. And to create a "who is and who is not" Na- tive Barrier. Art brings people together, it holds history, stories. It holds culture. I will mention that I teach my art classes to federally recognized and state recog- nized people. I wonder sometimes how the federal artist would feel if I stopped teaching these classes and tried to exclude them from traditions the way they con- tinue to try to exclude everyone else. But I continue to tell myself that that isn't the traditional way to act, and I refuse to stoop to that level.

I read a testimony that was upset about Federal artists selling next to someone who is state recognized. What it comes down to in that case is art quality. A federal tribal artist has nothing to fear from a state artist, unless their quality is less and vice versa. This is because, they're both Indian in the eyes of the law. The hierarchy needs to stop. What about the Hispanic people who are now selling beadwork at pow wows and are assumed to be Native American. They are copying our northern art and selling it when they should be selling their beautiful traditional Aztec arts. To me this is more of a threat than another recognized artist selling.

As a tribal artist my first responsibility is to ensure the art is passed on and the tradition is not lost. Secondly it is currently my only source of income. Thirdly I am a state recognized native and currently the thought of discrediting state recognized tribes would truly be a loss to so many arts and crafts. I am one of maybe 5 wampum weavers left. I currently only know of one wampum weaver in Cherokee Nation, although I have taught many Cherokee Nation Citizens, none have taken up the art to the extent that I have yet several members of my tribe are now excelling in making these historic belts and straps.

I get bullied because I am a state recognized artist, I get harassed. I am immediately discredited and my work must be three times as accurate as the federal tribal artists. This is what I deal with when I go to sell my art on a daily basis. The only protection I have is the Arts and Craft act of 1990 for my quality art that is getting harder and harder to find.

State recognized people have few rights, the right to our identity is one of them.

The right to say our art is Native made is accurate and granted by Federal law. I appreciate your time to hear my testimony. You are welcome to e-mail me at any time or contact me through *www.cherokeespirits.com* if you require further input or wish to look at my art which the federal tribes wish to revoke protections for.

Thank you.

PREPARED STATEMENT OF ELOISE JOSEY, EXECUTIVE DIRECTOR, ALABAMA INDIAN AFFAIRS COMMISSION

I appreciate the opportunity to testify regarding the Modernizing of the Indian Arts and Crafts Act.

The State of Alabama recognizes nine (9) tribal governments. Eight of these tribes are state-recognized and one (the Poarch Band of Creek Indians) is federally recognized. In 1984, the Alabama Legislature created the Alabama Indian Affairs Commission recognizing seven (7) tribal governments granting authority to the Commission Board to set up criteria for recognizing any further groups. Two additional groups were recognized by the Board in 2001 following that criteria, which is in the Administrative Code for the State of Alabama.

The Commission consists of representatives from each of the tribal governments, one Senator appointed by the Lt. Governor, one State Representative appointed by the Speaker of the House, one Federally-Recognized Indian person living in Alabama (not Poarch Creek) and one representative appointed by the Board.

The Alabama Indian Affairs Commission supports the modernizing of the Indian Arts and Crafts Law and supports strengthening the ability to enforce this Act as it should be. The Commission office, as well as, State government works to make sure that this Law is adhered to. This office has requested and continues to request the publication regarding the Indian Arts and Craft Law (from the Department of Interior) in order to disseminate to every Mayor in Alabama, and every Indian tribe holding Pow Wows or Festivals where Indian art might be sold. In a further attempt to support the Indian Arts and Craft Act, the Commission will be introducing legislation to further strengthen the ability to make sure that any events held in Alabama adhere to the Indian Arts and Craft Act.

I do not believe that the definition of who an Indian artisan is should be changed. It states quite clearly that "Indian is defined as a member of a federally or officially State recognized Tribe, or a certified Indian artisan"; and the definition of Indian Tribe as "Any federally recognized Indian Tribe, Band, Nation, Alaska. . ." and "Any Indian group that has been formally recognized as an Indian Tribe by a State Legislature, a State Commission, or another similar organization. . .".

There will always be people who will try to circumvent the law. These people could be impersonating a federally-recognized Indian, a state-recognized Indian, or a certified Indian artisan. To ignore state-recognized tribes simply to make things easier is not the answer. Again, the State of Alabama and the Alabama Indian Affairs Commission will continue in our endeavors to enforce the Indian Arts and Crafts Act.

Thank you for this opportunity to share the concerns of Alabama's Indian people.

PREPARED STATEMENT OF HON. HERMAN G. HONANIE, CHAIRMAN, HOPI TRIBE

Dear Senators Udall and Heinrich,

Thank you for the Field Hearing of Senate Committee on Indian Affairs at the Santa Fe Indian School on July 7, 2017, titled Cultural Sovereignty Series: Modernizing the Indian Arts and Crafts Act to Honor Native Identity and Expression. The Hopi Tribe appreciates your support for the Hopi Tribe and other tribes in our efforts to protect and preserve our cultural heritage and artisans from fake Hopi Arts and Crafts. Therefore, on behalf of the Hopi Tribe and the Hopi people, I offer our strong support for modernizing the Indian Arts and Crafts Act to honor Native identity and expression.

Hopi people trace our history back thousands of years, making Hopi one of the oldest living cultures in the world. Today, Hopi is a vibrant, living culture. Hopi people, *Hopisinom*, continue to perform our ceremonial and traditional responsibilities in our ancient language.

At Hopi, giving has been at the heart of our society and social compact since time immemorial. The very cornerstone of Hopi society and sociality is the exchange of mutually beneficial gifts, and relationships reconfigured by those exchanges. Gifts are communications in a language of social belonging, and giving is reciprocal, binding individuals and groups to each other and the spiritual realm. The honor of giving means respecting and honoring both the giver and the recipient.

Hopi arts and crafts are an adaptation to the outside world of expressions of our culture. However, we face a recurring threat that strikes at the heart of our culture and economy. We understand the problem of imitation Hopi arts and crafts. Hopi culture is regularly misinterpreted and misrepresented by non-Hopi people for commercial purposes including the continuing sale of fake Hopi arts and crafts.

Pursuant to the Indian Arts and Crafts Act we continually work with the Indian Arts and Crafts Board to address this problem in the United States. However, we also understand that this problem extends internationally, literally around the world.

Therefore, we share the concerns expressed in the testimony of Joyce Begay Foss, Director, Living Traditions Education Center, Museum of Indian Arts and Culture and Navajo weaver regarding authenticity and cultural affiliation. We agree that authentic Navajo rugs are Navajo made, and Navajo rugs made by non-Native people or non-Navajo Native people are not authentic.

Authentic Hopi *Katsina* dolls are made exclusively by Hopi people and not non-Hopi people, including Native people such as Navajo people or people from other tribes. Although the Indian Arts and Crafts Act and Board has offered us some support in the misappropriation of Hopi culture by non-Native people and in addressing this frustrating and recurrent problem, our regular objections are only honored in cases of non-Native people. The current Indian Arts and crafts Act is a truth in marketing law does not apply to non-Hopi Native people who create likenesses of Hopi *Katsina* dolls. Imitation Hopi *Katsina* dolls made by non-Hopi Native people are considered legal under the existing Act.

Further, the generic and liberal use of the Hopi term "Kachina" by non-Hopi Native people, such as Navajo people or people of other tribes, as well as non-Native people further contributes to misleading marketing of clearly imitation art arts and crafts.

Therefore, to protect the authenticity of our Hopi tribal heritage, we recommend the Senate Committee on Indian Affairs and Indian Arts and Crafts Board direct its efforts and attention to truth in marketing culturally and tribally authentic arts and crafts through the Indian Arts and Crafts Act, which is currently a truth in marketing law addressing Native Americans collectively.

We agree that it is important for law enforcement to prioritize its resources on prosecuting those who knowingly counterfeit Native American art and craftwork, and that to accomplish this effectively, federal law needs to provide the necessary tools to investigate and prosecute those who exploit and undermine the cultural heritage of Native Americans.

Therefore we also support the testimony of all the witnesses at the hearing, and fully support the testimony Damon Martinez, Former U.S. Attorney for New Mexico, that laid out seven recommendations for modernizing the current law to reflect the needs of Native American communities. Specifically, to make the law more comprehensive and effective, we support:

> First, that the Act should consider the importation of Native American-style merchandise into the commerce of the United States separately from the sale of Native American-style merchandise in the United States.

> Second, the Act should require clearly and simply that Native American-style merchandise

imported into the United States must have an indelible country-of-origin marking.

Third, the Act should require that the seller of Native American-style merchandise in the United States have a basis for representing that such merchandise is actually Native American produced.

Fourth, the Act should have a specific forfeiture section.

Fifth, Laundering of monetary instruments, 18 USC 1956, should be amended to include a violation of Misrepresentation of Indian produced goods and products, 18 USC 1159, as a specified unlawful activity.

Sixth, Authorization for interception of wire, oral, or electronic communications, 18 USC 2116, should be amended to include Misrepresentation of Indian produced goods and products, 18 USC 1159, as an offense for investigation

And finally, the Department of Homeland Security should be encouraged to flag or seize during customs inspections Native American-style merchandise imported into the commerce of the United States that does not have an indelible country-of-origin marking on each item of merchandise.

This illicit trafficking of fake Hopi And Native American arts and crafts must stop. Therefore, the Hopi Tribe supports your current effort to modernize the Indian Arts and Crafts Act to honor Native identity and expression, which will strengthen tribes' ability to protect their artisan's arts and crafts, increase penalties and explicitly prohibit the marketing and trafficking of fake tribal arts and crafts.

PREPARED STATEMENT OF KATHI OUELLET, PRESIDENT, INDIAN ARTS AND CRAFTS ASSOCIATION

Dear Senator Udall,

As the President of the Indian Arts and Crafts Association, I'd like to respond to your July 7, 2017 hearing on updating the Indian Arts and Crafts Act.

The Indian Arts and Crafts Association is a non-profit organization based in Albuquerque, New Mexico. Our mission is to promote, preserve and protect authentic Native American arts and crafts. We also support and promote Native American artists, and support all aspects of the Indian Arts and Crafts industry from the material suppliers through the end consumers. The Indian Arts and Crafts Association has been in existence for over 40 years, and while most of our members are here in the US, we do have members in Japan, Germany, France and Australia.

The Indian Arts and Crafts Act is the foundation of our organization and our educational efforts to promote authentic Native American arts and crafts. Educating the general public, Native American artists, and retail and wholesale businesses is critical to maintaining and increasing economic opportunity for Native artists. The fraudulent art market affects every aspect of the Native American art industry, but has a particularly harsh economic effect on artists.

We fully support and encourage the modernization of the Indian Arts and Crafts Act. We hope that you will add specific language that addresses all aspects of the fraudulent art market including, Internet auction sites, web sites and social media. We also encourage you to increase civil and criminal penalties as deterrents. Specifically, we hope that language will be added that aggregates the total of non-authentic properties seized, so that it is not the dollar value, but rather the simple violation of the Act that triggers civil or criminal prosecution at the Federal level. We also hope that a forfeiture clause be added. Given the dollar value of the fraudulent goods being brought into the US, we believe that the current fines are treated as a "cost of doing business" rather than a true deterrent.

In addition, while we would like to see a requirement to indelibly mark all imports with the country of origin. We understand that this issue is complicated and expensive, and although we believe that this could significantly reduce fraudulent goods being brought into the U.S., at this point we recommend study in Trademarks, Copyrights and indelible import marks, so as not to hold up the implementation of other critical parts of the modernization.

The Indian Arts and Crafts Association works very closely with the Indian Arts and Crafts Board, and supports its efforts to increase the economic opportunity of Native American artists. The services that the Board provides are invaluable to our members and therefore the preservation of Native American heritage and culture. The Board publishes and distributes brochures, conducts workshops to help artists, and provides information about current laws. The Indian Arts and Crafts Association appreciates our relationship with the Board, and we are fully committed to support and approve legislation going forward to modernize the Act.

———

PREPARED STATEMENT OF DAVID S. MONTGOMERY, CHEROKEE NATION OF OKLAHOMA TRIBAL MEMBER

Dear Senators Hoeven and Udall,

My name is David Montgomery. I am of Cherokee and Choctaw descent, and I am a registered tribal member of Cherokee Nation of Oklahoma, one of the three federally-recognized Cherokee tribes. I have many friends and family who are artists and registered tribal members of various federally-recognized tribes in Oklahoma, New Mexico, California and throughout Indian Country.

I was very pleased your committee visited Santa Fe for a Field Hearing on Modernizing the Indian Arts and Crafts Act (IACA) on July 7th 2017, and I was happy to be in attendance at this important hearing.

I believe it is long overdue to modernize the 1990 IACA, and help protect Indian artists of federally-recognized tribes, as well as maintain the sovereignty of federally-recognized tribes to determine who is and who is not a member of their tribal nations.

I know I speak for many Indian artists who would like the IACA to be updated to remove state-recognized tribes from the language of the law. As has been acknowledged by all federally-recognized tribes and several states facing the question of "state-recognition" of supposed tribes within their borders, it has long been determined that tribal recognition and issues concerning Indian tribes is the exclusive domain of the Federal government since the earliest days of the republic, and covered under the Commerce Clause of the U.S. Constitution.

What many federally-recognized tribes have now observed since 1990 is an explosion of groups of individuals claiming to be "tribes" in various states (most notably Southern states such as Alabama, Georgia, Louisiana, South Carolina, etc), seeking and obtaining "state-recognition". The process for vetting "tribes" at the state-level for recognition is non-uniform and non-rigorous compared to the federal recognition process, and varies widely from state to state. It can be simply a "governor proclamation" (hardly the intent of the rigor expected for the IACA), or some state-level office on Indian affairs that lacks the stringency for tribal recognition that is used at the Federal level. Regardless, state-level recognition of Indian tribes as sovereigns and their members as "Indians" oversteps the bounds for recognition of sovereign entities that resides solely at the Federal level.

As an example of the potential for corruption and circumvention of the existing IACA law, some state-recognized "tribes" simply ask for an annual fee (anywhere from $15–$50 dollars) and one can "join" the tribe, with no rigor in their registration process such as genealogical trees for descent from an Indian ancestor, state-certified birth, death and adoption certificates, etc. This also neglects the fact that most state-recognized tribes lack any historic record of connection to the tribe of Indians they are claiming to be, and state-tribes that have applied for federal-recognition with the BIA have been rejected because there was simply no burden of proof to support their claims as Indian tribes.

To remedy this, I propose the following:

1) removal of "state-recognized tribes" from the language of the IACA

2) certification of an individual by a federally-recognized tribe as being an "Indian artist". This path would allow authentic tribal descendants, who may not be able to register as a tribal member but are deemed by the tribe to be authentic descendants of that tribe, to become certified as "Indian artists" and thus protected under the revised IACA. This path preserves the Federal government's sole authority to recognize Indian tribes, preserves the sovereignty of federally-recognized tribes to determine who is and who is not a member of their tribe, and preserves sovereignty for tribes to acknowledge their non-member descendants as certified Indian artists in order for those non-enrolled individuals to be protected under the IACA.

PREPARED STATEMENT OF HON. BILL JOHN BAKER, PRINCIPAL CHIEF, CHEROKEE NATION

Dear Chairman Hoeven and Vice-Chairman Udall:

Please accept the following letter in response to the Committee's recent oversight field hearing on "Modernizing the Indian Arts and Crafts Act to Honor Native Identity and Expression." I ask that these thoughts be made part of the hearing record.

The Cherokee Nation strongly urges the Committee to closely examine the Federal Indian Arts and Crafts Act, and, where appropriate, consider legislative changes that will better guarantee the authenticity of true American Indian art. We believe a modernized law, enforced and regulated by the Indian Arts and Crafts Board, will benefit all federally recognized tribes and their artisans and ensure greater accountability in this area.

From the perspective of the Cherokee Nation, "Indian art" is art made by a citizen of a federally recognized tribe. Under current law, however, artists, tribes, and organizations falsely claim legitimacy or Native heritage in order to sell Indian art. These deceptive practices perpetrate the art sales and art markets across Indian Country.

The current definition of "Indian" within the law is far too broad. "Indian art" must be limited to true Indian artists. And again, we believe true Indian artists are those that are citizens of federally recognized tribes. The Committee must strengthen the law to protect these artists, and ensure that fraudulent artists and sellers are penalized.

To achieve this goal, the Committee must eliminate protections for state recognized tribes.

As you know, Oklahoma is home to 38 federally recognized tribes and outside of Alaska has the highest percentage of Native people (approximately 13 percent). Last year the Oklahoma state legislature considered and approved a new Indian arts bill, one that strengthens existing law and embodies the spirit of what it means to be "Indian" in Oklahoma.

The new law closes a "state recognized tribe" loophole and better protects Oklahoma Indian artists and the integrity and authenticity of Indian art in our state. Now, in order to sell Indian art you must be a citizen of a federally recognized tribe. Oklahoma tribes, museums, and individual artists unified behind this legislation and supported its passage.

A stronger act ensures ultimately consumer protection. It protects buyers who want to buy authentic Indian art. It also protects our Indian artists. In Oklahoma, they are a small but invaluable community and commodity for our state. We have a responsibility to advocate for them and be more proactive in defending the interests and rights of tribal governments and tribal citizens.

People who falsely claim to be Native or flood our communities with fake Indian art hurt the real Indian art industry. I applaud the Committee for holding this hearing, and encourage you to take the necessary steps to move toward a stronger and better enforceable Indian Arts and Crafts Act.

Thank you for your attention to this important issue.

ADDITIONAL LETTERS AND STATEMENTS SUBMITTED FOR THE RECORD

To whom it may concern:

As a citizen of the Echota Cherokee Tribe Of AL, I appreciate your work on the Arts and Craft Law and join with the Alabama Indian Affairs Commission in support of its strengthening. I implore you to maintain the definition of 'Indian' set forth in the present law, and to continue the inclusion of the state recognized tribes.

Thank you in advance for your consideration of this matter.

Sincerely,
Deborah Davis

I was in Santa Fe last week and saw reproduction Native American jewelry all around the Plaza. One way to identify a business
selling Asian made jewelry is to notice how bright the lights are inside the store. Lots of glass cases and too much light wattage is a dead giveaway. Why don't you clean up that area and shut those people down?

Glenn White, Scottsdale, Arizona

———

I support Senator Udall's proposal to modernize and enforce the livelihood of fellow Native Artist and their communities from Fraud
Thank you

Jesse Salcedo

———

This is my statement and no way am I speaking for anyone but myself, but hope my concerns fall on open ears.
First of all; we need all our artist where they be Federal or State-without all of them our culture, like our people die out-Their erpertise in the making and use of all natural materials and animals, not excluding anything from turtles/fish/trees and plants are needed.
I am a local NA artist from Alabama where most of my cherokee ancestors lived, until the removal act was put in force.I try to use any and or all natural things the creator gave us to better my life and support myself and family. My bloodline comes down from Moytoy 1st through Robert Cherokee Thomas and his daughter Ann Martha Tiny bird Cherokee-
My Ancestors were proud and resourceful people. They shared all they knew for future generations to survive and make use of if they chose.. They took from the earth what was needed and shared or traded items and their knowledge, to support them and family, letting others do the same. A lot of my living is making and selling items from beads to furs and hide, learning from
those who teach it to me, and sharing this to others especially the younger generation (Our Future)in hopes our culture and Heritage does not die, as it almost has many times before-It is the Local State Artist in rural areas, that has opened the door for young people to see what in truth, our past was like, NOT what was taught in school- and to teach them about keeping it true, for the future-Many of my Ancestors have long gone and with just enough to pass down what they knew with me to survive and pass on with this generation.I am one of few who has kept this interest and hope to open the ears of others- If the State Recognized Tribes are cast aside and not allowed to Be/make, sell or trade same items as large companies and or Federal tribes-How are we to teach our arts/crafts and culture to others and survive?Not everyone has Internet or TV-But the ones who do mostly see the fake items passed off as Hand Made NA crafts, on Ebay or sites like Etsy, which in reality comes from China and other foreign countries.Many letters have been sent to try and stop this but falls on deft ears. How do we show how all parts of deer or shells of turtles and plants were used to make clothes and rattles to use in our spiritual ceremonies and gatherings or everyday use? and or give joy to those both seeing, wearing and using these items that they made?WE TEACH HOW-People like to see in person arts and crafts that are hand made-Why it is so important that local artist and teachers survive. Showing our children may keep interest in our culture; If these rights are not taken away, and not taught because for lack of interest?. Every State has its own rules now of what you can gather or use unless you carry a card from a recognized tribe, and then it is closely watched.Federal tribes and large companies, have tried to do away with State Artist and tribes for a long time and I have seen more and more items from China made from artificial materials, passed off as NA art coming from commercial companies at a lot of pow wows or gatherings, A lot of our people meet to share ideas and sell or trade their hand made crafts at these gatherings-The State Artist I know work hard to teach and promote the use of all items given of mother nature for our use, and spiritual being ,giving back to their people and tribe.We need our State as well as Federal tribes to promote the growth and culture of our people. Since most are far apart. But we are limited to what and how much we can use, depending on State you are from and items you use to make your art, like bear claws and hides that come more from our Northern States, or Quahog shells that comes from the coast that was part of our culture for so long. and becoming more hard to find the good color that was once all along the clear waters, and with our waters poisoned with pollutants and forrest cut down, that helped us have fresh and healthy air and animals, now most is all gone.Fish and skin drumheads to use in our drums to make our hearts sore with

Eagles as we dance and wear their feathers. Are becoming much harder to find what was once plentiful.Forrest is taken away to make large cities, animals have no where to go or live. So materials from there are harder to come by.The ones that are, is usually just thrown on side of road or in a ditch from trophy hunters, just using the head, instead of offering rest to artist or families for food .If we are excluded from making and selling our wares at gatherings or stores; then our culture may be doomed, jobs to support our family gone, and more poverty taking control. I ask for the sake of my forefathers to not exclude State Tribes in this or other hearings, in being able to do and have the same right as Federal Tribes, or big companies. Most of us carry the same blood and need our rights to survive. Thank you for listening.

Bob Upton

Ladies & Gentlemen,

I fully support Tom Udall's efforts to strengthen the Indian Arts & Crafts Act of 1990 to further protect our Native American Art.

In a time when too many of the items available for purchase are "Made in China" it becomes imperative to protect the quality of all American products. Strengthening this Act is one step out of many which I hope will be taken.

Protected Native American Art gives "Made in America" something we can be proud of.

Thank you for your effort on behalf of our National Treasures.

Sincerely,

PATRICIA J. WITT,
Marathon, FL.

Over the years, I have heard Native artists complain about their work being copied. Their works are inspired by their culture and the lives they have lived. Natives are expressing their innermost thoughts through their art. It's a personal expression not felt by those who copy. Those who are copying the Native artists are stealing a culture and potential income.

I have also known people who have purchased and treasured art works they assumed were created by Native artists, but were not. The Indian Arts & Crafts Association's logo ensures the art work is created by a Native artist. The IACA requires documentation from the tribe and examples of the artist's work before including the artist in their registry. One of the problems has been the lack of funding for promoting the work the IACA has done and making potential buyers aware of what to look for when purchasing Native art.

The bigger problem has been punishing those who knowingly copy Native art for profit. Even if the fakes have been found and reported, the laws protecting Native art are not always enforced. I believe this is due, in part, to limited Federal funding dedicated to this area.

I have been an arts administrator for over 20 years and an artist for many more years, and I have felt the sorry artists feel when there work has been copied, particularly when they are not acknowledged or have not benefitted from financial compensation. I have also been honored to be an artist member of the IACA.

CHRISTINE KLIMMEK, BS ART EDUCATION
Oneida Nation Arts Program Coordinator

Dear Sir:

I recommend the following:

Only tribal members who are officially enrolled in a federally recognized tribe or state recognized be authorized to sale items as an authentic Indigenous/American Indian craft or art product.

Proof must be provided by the craftsman/craftswoman as an officially enrolled member of either a federal or state recognized tribe.

All Indigenous/American Indian craft or art work must be created and verified to have been done only within the USA.

I am enrolled with the Echota Cherokee Tribe of Alabama.

I was appointed to the Board of Directors for the Florida Governor's Council on Indian Affairs for the state of Florida.

I am a past member of The Board of Directors for the Vietnam Era Veterans Inter-Tribal Association, Inc.

I am a member of the Presidential Advisory Board for President Trump.

I will be advising President Trump on all issues related to Indigenous/American Indians and tribal government issues.

What is your relationship with Secretary Ryan Zinke? Have you included the BIA in this review of the Craft and Arts issue?

I recommend that you send a formal notice to the following:

All federal tribes

All state recognized tribes

All commissions of Indian affairs

Provide a federal list for all federal tribes and state recognized tribes that are authorized to make and sale craft and or Art as Indigenous/American Indian made solely inside the USA

Sincerely,

JOEL K. HARRIS, SR., PH.D.
Ocala, FL.

————

Good morning members of the Committee,

My name is Steve K. Boone, I am a member of the Zuni Pueblo Indian Tribe.

I would like to submit a comment concerning the Indian Arts and Crafts Act, which is vital for all gifted Native American artisans. More is needed to disceminate a large variety of the authenticity and quality of hand crafted designs that symbolize importance and meanings to each tribal nation across the Americas. By developing better educational efforts with the artisan and tribal leadership for all visitors who enter each region of where they could find and purchase the unique products for their appreciation, along with knowing they were handcrafted by an individual of an American Indian.

Best regards.

————

As a collector of genuine Native American art, I hope you not only continue the current level of enforcement and preferably provide an increased level of surveillance to ensure that authenic goods are being sold.

I have been several galleries in Santa Fe when they have been trying to sell goods of dubious origin to visitors.

It seemed to me at that time that this was short term thinking since if folks think they have been cheated, they are less likely to return to New Mexico, however for some making a buck is the immediate goal.

PATRICK BLACKWELL

————

Dear Senator Udall,

I am in favor of legislation that will support the livelihoods of Native artists, while also protecting Native artists and all Native Americans and their communities from fraudulent practices.

Thank you.

CHARLES T. SAUNDERS, PH.D, ACG, ALB,
Franklin University—Columbus, OH

————

Thank you for conducting the recent hearing in Santa Fe on proposed legislation to strengthen enforcement of the Indian Arts and Crafts Act of 1990. I support your work to protect the livelihoods of Native artists and defend Native communities from fraudulent practices.

KARIE LUIDENS

————

Respectfully, Native makers of Native art should be the decision-makers on their wares.

Sen. Udall's proposal to update the Indian Arts and Crafts Act of 1990 comes at a time when theft and fraud seems to be more sophisticated than ever.

In New Mexico, we've learned there's a need to protect our chiles and laws are now in place.

It's time the U.S. improve protections on all Native products.

Sincerely,

SUSAN BORTZ-JOHNSON,
Cedar Crest, NM.

———

My name is James S. de Champlon, for the past 10 years I have worked with the Cultural Services Department of the City of Albuquerque as the Historic Old Town Portal Market Manager. The Portal Market is a multicultural arts and crafts market that is open year round, and though not limited to Native American artisans, a majority of the participants in the program are Native Americans.

Over time it has become apparent to me that the Indian Arts and Crafts Act in its efforts to promote Native American artisans could use some kind of reinforcement in order to become more effective in achieving this goal and so I was excited to hear about the Senate Indian Affairs Committee efforts towards Modernizing the Indian Arts and Crafts Act.

In my position as Portal Market manager I work with both Native American artisans along with artisans of other varied cultural backgrounds and it has been by experience that similar issues of, authenticity in production, and materials are shared by all of the artisans that participate in the Portal Market program and perhaps in the arts and crafts industry as a whole.

I have developed some ideas about how the IACA might be reinforced, specifically thru the provision that relates to the establishment of trade marks and the possibility of broadening the scope of such a system so that it might include other arts and crafts categories related to various aspects of regional and ethnic heritage from both domestic and foreign artisans along with a differentiation between categories such as traditional, contemporary, and manufactured items.

I would be happy to share my thoughts in more detail if the Committee might find it useful.

Thank you for your efforts.

———

Hello,

I'm French, and looking for authentic Native American Indian Arts and Crafts to sell to Museums shops in France and in Europe.

My last visit to the USA was in April 2016 and I saw in Santa Fe, Taos, Gallup. . . (even in Albuquerque airport) many items sold as Navajo pottery, Pueblo pottery, Zuni fetishes, Hopi kachinas. . .etc. . .which were obviously not authentic and not locally produced (looking like they were coming from the Far East and Middle East).

Some of these items end up in European shops, and sometimes even in Museum shops.

Just thinking that a testimony from across the ocean would be beneficial in strenghtening the Act enforcement and maintain the quality and authenticity of Native works of art.

Staying at your disposal.

Sincerely,

OLIVIER LUCOTTE.

———

Our retail store Ownership and Management at Lantern Dancer, in Pagosa Springs, CO, supports Senator Udall's modernization proposal of the Indian Arts and Crafts Act. Specifically, we want to increase the capability to enforce compliance to the act and education and outreach to artists, organizations, businesses, and the general public. We also know it is critically important to address the selling of authentic Native American arts and crafts via the Internet and Social Media. We work direct with Calvin Begay and have been impacted by the influx of fraudulent and fake works.

Thank you for helping us help protect our artists and our retail business.

Sincerely,

LEANNE GOEBEL,
Manager/Board member IACA

———

I fully support efforts to enhance and enforce legislation providing harsher penalties for those who would cheat our indigenous artists by appropriating their culture. As a retail member of the Indian Arts and Crafts Association, I know fakes hurt all of us. They take unfair advantage of the artists, the dealers and the unsuspecting consumers who unknowingly help perpetuate this fraud by their pur-

chases. Penalties for producing fake Native American art or dealing in it must be stronger and must be rigidly enforced.
Thank you for your consideration.

SUZIE MCKAY,
Indigenous Arts, LLC.

———

Hello,

I'm emailing in support of Senator Tom Udall's proposal to submit a new bill to modernize the Indian Arts and Crafts Act of 1990. I am in favor of his proposed legislation to strengthen the Act's enforcement, to support the livelihoods of Native artists and protecting Native communities from fraudulent practices.
Hope this helps.

———

I support the modernization of the Indian Arts and Crafts Act, especially the aggregation and forfeiture issues. Also, we need an increase in the capability in enforcement and education and outreach to Native artists, organizations, businesses and the general public interested in buying and selling authentic Native art.
Sincerely,

DAWN DUNKELBERGER,
Aka Dawn Dark Mountain

———

Dear Senator Udall:

I follow Indian Arts and Crafts for my own love of the art of Native Americans. One of the websites that I frequently utilize is Shumakolowa Native Arts in Albuquerque, New Mexico. This modernization is vitally important to protect the artifacts of native peoples for so many native artists; archeologists, and to provide clear and authoritative directions on how Indian Arts and Crafts should be handled.

I did my homework before I selected two reliable, authentic & reputable artists' distributors who feature work in specific areas: jewelry. pottery, art, instruments; media, pendletons and other woven items; carvings, baskets, rugs. There are here in the Bay Area many buyers who go into a store that sells turquoise jewelry which is not authenticated. Who kniws what they are really getting when they buy an Indian necklace. Shumakolawa authenticates every art piece they distribute to a buyer. And the case of stolen artifacts has become quite serious. Dishonest collectors are stealing valuable artifacts and selling them on the black market. This is a case of stealing the heritage of Native Americans.

This law needs to be strengthened to reflect the changing circumstances that Native Americans are facing to support their culture and share their priceless artifacts with others through museums; reputable distributors and private collectors.

I can attest that Native American jewelry is filled with so much life and so many activities that the jewelry symbolizes.
Sincerely yours,

REBECCA HAZLEWOOD,
El Cerrito, CA.

———

I whole heartedly support your proposal to update and modernize the Indian Arts and Crafts Act, and support better protections for Native American artists and craftspeople.
Thank you,

JOHN LANDRY

———

Thank you for supporting the new updated legislation proposed by Udall to protect the Native American Art and Crafts.

CAROLYN RODRIGUEZ,
Albuquerque, NM.

———

Senator Udall please help us keep the Arts law as it currently is and keep the interests of State recognized tribes in good standing. I am not an artisan but I am friends and a tribal brother to several who are and they are every bit Native Craftsmen. Thank you for your involvement

MIKE RICHARDS,
Echota Cherokee.

———

Dear Honorable,

The present efforts are to be commended, and continued, thank you. The present focus is on Items being made out of the USA and being brought into the USA and being sold as handmade/handcrafted American Indian Art. This practice needs continued enforcement.

There are over 1,000 jewelry factories in Albuquerque, NM, that are also creating American Indian style jewelry. Mostly Navajo style jewelry. The Jewelry is sold retail and wholesale to shops/galleries around the country and world markets. These businesses have been very active since before the 1950's. many of them have been and are members of the Indian Arts and Crafts Association. These Businesses have created this association the IACA. These businesses have wholesale/retail shows several times a year. Shops that buy from these Factories have a IACA label/sticker placed appropriately in their shops/stores, in America and Internationally. The IACA claims that all items sold by their businesses are American Indian Handmade/handcrafted. The authentication of each business member and their items for sale as American Indian Handmade/handcrafted items is based solely upon their application and acceptance into the IACA organization. No evaluation process to authenticate the items to see if American Indians are making the Items is done. The IACA sticker is placed in the shops and the customers feel confident that all items in these shops are handcrafted/Handmade by American Indians. These factory business also contract with award winning Indian Artists and use their designs to create jewelry. These manufactured jewelry pieces have been sold on TV home shopping markets in the past. The artist is brought on the show explaining how they handcraft/Handmake each piece. The pieces are massed produced by these factories and are sold on these tv shows. Mass production is their method of meeting the demand of their world market American Indian styled jewelry and products. So not all American Indian Style Jewelry is made overseas. The IACA is a great place to check for enforcing the present law.

Creating the next generations of laws has to include the complete transparency of these companies in Albuquerque and Gallup, New Mexico and other places in the region. These companies pay no taxes for selling wholesale. The people who buy their products and sell at shows pay no taxes. The loss of tax monies over the years since the beginning including the beginning of IACA, is in the billions.

Loloma,

BENNARD DALLASVUYAOMA,
Nephew of Charles Loloma.

———

Good morning. I am writing in regards to the revision of the Indian Arts and Crafts Act. After watching the testimonies given, there are some concerns that the definition of what is "Indian" will remove state recognized tribes. I have concerns as I am a tribal citizen of the Echota Cherokee Tribe of Alabama. Because the 3 federal tribes only use two (of many) rolls listing Cherokees, my family cannot enroll in a federal tribe. However, my DNA shows North, South and Central American Indian markers. My genealogy also shows Cherokee, Shawnee and Catawba ancestors. Yet, I cannot enroll in any of the federal tribes. There are thousands of people just like myself who are truly Native American, Their only option is to join a state recognized tribe or not be enrolled at all. This does not make us any less Native American.

I would like to see the board pull from all three definitions of "Indian" and have all three participate in these discussion. It is unfair that only federal tribal members were included in the testimonies. Under the Act, "an Indian is defined as a member of any Federally or officially State recognized Indian Tribe, or an individual certified as an Indian artisan by an Indian Tribe."

Please consider a full representation of all Native Americans when addressing these issues by having federal, state and certified artisans in the decisionmaking process.

Best regards.

WEEYA MICHELLE SMITH.

———

The American Indian Alaska Native Tourism Association (AIANTA) promotes economic development and cultural perpetuation in Indian Country through its mission: to define, introduce, grow and sustain American Indian, Alaska Native and Native Hawaiian tourism that honors traditions and values. Cultural tourism creates jobs and supports the teaching of each tribal nation's distinct food, language, art, music, dance and cultural practices across generations.

The Indian Arts and Crafts Board (IACB) has partnered with AIANTA to present consumer information, marketing information and protections available to tribal artists and to educate various publics about authentic tribal arts and crafts.

Art and crafts are integral to tribal cultures and heritage and represent important sources of revenue for tribal members and their families. AIANTA supports strengthening enforcement of the Indian Arts and Crafts Act through changing laws to allow for an aggregation of individual transactions that would enable federal prosecutors to more effectively prosecute largescale distributors who violate the Act. We also support more education and training of local, state and federal enforcement officers and increased funding for investigations, especially in the areas of Internet sales and making sure imports of Native American-style arts and crafts are indelibly marked with the country of origin.

Tourist and other consumers' confidence in the purchase of authentic American Indian arts are essential to authentic tribal tourism. Consumer education materials by the Indian Arts and Crafts Board educates visitors to Indian Country and gives them confidence in their purchases.

We commend Senator Tom Udall and the Senate Committee on Indian Affairs for taking up this important strengthening of the Arts and Crafts Act

CAMILLE FERGUSON,
Executive Director, American Indian Alaska Native Tourism Association

————

Dear Senator Udall,

I am president of the Santa Fe Downtown Merchants association, board Secretary and ex board chair of SWAIA, and a business owner in Santa Fe.

I have cooperated with the IACB for over 17 years trying to stop the shameless miscreants in our own community as they cheat, lie, defraud, and commit cultural genocide with relative impunity since you left the Attorney General's office. In fairness,other Attorneys' General have tried, the Fish and Wildlife and other Interior people have tried as well, but the local corruption on every level and the greed of dealers, and even Native artists who also sometime lie about their materials and methods just gets worse and worse.

Clearly, underfunding is the biggest issue, but following close on its heels is legitimate fear of these threatening and violent people, their very public bragging about paying off elected and appointed public officials, and their equally public display of stocks of automatic firearms, unsavory connections, and willingness to hurt others.

Hopefully, bigger fines, increased enforcement, and more visible educational possibilities might help. Santa Fe's new "authenticity zone" is an interesting idea, but carries with it no enforcement capability or intent. I simply hope that making some one sign a pledge will make it easier for the AG Balderas to prove that such a person was aware of the rules when he broke them.

I wish that you had had more time to meet with those of us who actually live and work amidst this retail situation, and would recommend that you or your staff visit with me, with John Dressman, Mark Bahti, and some others as we are in a situation to see this entire dynamic play out "where the rubber meets the road".

When a subset of local merchants is determined, in Santa Fe, in Scottsdale, in Gallup, or in Las Vegas to defraud consumers, cheat natives, and destroy a way of life, seemingly without retribution, it is alarming.

We have tried to help in the past, and would like to do more.

Enforcement, secret shoppers, and increased attention to money laundering, bribery, and other nefarious activities all require money, I suspect that is the eternal crux of the matter. Perhaps this could be sold as a form of enhanced border security.

The IACB and other Interior personnel are dedicated, smart, determined, and overtasked. Again, I guess that's money.

Thank you.

ELIZABETH MCNALLY PETTUS,
Things Finer, Santa Fe, New Mexico

————

I am writing in support of Senator Tom Udall's proposal to submit a new bill to modernize the Indian Arts and Crafts Act of 1990. My wife and I have a small collection of authentic Indian arts and crafts and greatly treasure them. I am pleased to hear that the proposed legislation will strengthen the Act's enforcement, supporting the livelihoods of Native artists and protecting Native communities from fraudulent practices.

I have seen several locations selling items that were being passed as authentic. We have studied this art enough to note some inauthentic pieces being passed as authentic, and believe that if there is one piece on the shelf is fraudulent, they all are suspect. However, we have watched as other people bought these pieces believing them to be authentic, including jewelry, textiles (blankets) and pottery.

This law needs stronger teeth and greater enforcement. Please stiffen the penalties and increase the enforcement so severely against fake Indian art that this fraudulent practice is not worth what these "con artists" will lose.

JOE AND STEPHANIE CAVANAUGH

———

I urge you to take measures to strengthen the Indian Arts and Crafts Act of 1990. I have been a longtime purchaser and collector of Native American art and jewelry. Our native artists have faced an onslaught of cheap foreign producers flooding the market with knockoffs and imitations.

Unfortunately, many people associate Indian jewelry with cheaply produced items, many of which are mass-produced overseas with fake turquoise and other materials. This cheats both consumers and producers. Additionally, labels used to identify native art are confusing.

These practices undercut local markets, local jobs, and local economies as well as deceive consumers. High quality native artwork commands top dollar because of the skill and artistry involved as well as the uniqueness of the product. Many of us are more than willing to purchase American Indian art, handicrafts, and jewelry at fair market value, ensuring that the products are both authentic and priced to reflect fair market wages.

Please develop ways to better protect American jobs and local economies through labeling, enforcement, and other measures to ensure the authenticity of Native American arts and crafts.

Thank you.

CYNTHIA F. VAN DER WIELE
Durham, NC.

www.ingramcontent.com/pod-product-compliance
Lightning Source LLC
Chambersburg PA
CBHW081845250726
48659CB00008B/2613